A Status of Adivasis / Indigenous Peoples Land Series – 3

MAHARASHTRA

Brian Lobo

A Status of Adivasis/Indigenous Peoples Land Series – 3 : MAHARASHTRA
Brian Lobo

First Published, 2011

ISBN 978-93-5002-130-9

Published by
AAKAR BOOKS
28 E Pocket IV, Mayur Vihar Phase I, Delhi 110 091
Phone : 011 2279 5505 Telefax : 011 2279 5641
aakarbooks@gmail.com; www.aakarbooks.com

In association with
THE OTHER MEDIA
C 44, IInd Floor, Housing Society
South Extension Part I, New Delhi 110 049
Phones : 011 2462 9372/73 Fax : 011 4104 2271
Email : tom@theothermedia.org

Printed at
Mudrak, 30 A Patparganj, Delhi 110 091

Acknowledgements

The Status Report of Adivasis/Indigenous Peoples (SAIP) has been an important initiative of The Other Media and All India Coordinating Forum of Adivasis/Indigenous Peoples. It began with a lot of interest and enthusiasm with a wide consultation among activists, scholars and researchers interested in the Adivasis/Indigenous People's issues. However, the process seemed to have had its own pace and could not keep up with the expectation of completing the report on time. The present phase of the programme has covered, state-wise, issues of land and mining in the Adivasis/Indigenous People's areas.

This report on land issues in the Adivasi areas of Maharashtra has been prepared by Brian Lobo. We gratefully acknowledge the efforts made by the author and members of the Editorial Collective (EC) in preparing this report.

Members of the EC went through the report and gave their valuable comments and suggestions. We gratefully acknowledge their contribution that was available at every stage of preparation of the report. The efforts of the EC have been untiringly coordinated by C R Bijoy. The reports owe a lot to his relentless efforts to keep in the loop everyone concerned towards producing good results out of the reports. At the level of The Other Media, Ravi Hemadri, who worked as the Executive Director of the organisation through most part of the programme served as a link between the organisation and the EC. He continued to coordinate the final editing and printing of the reports. We gratefully acknowledge the role played by both C R Bijoy and Ravi Hemadri.

We acknowledge and thank the Adivasi Academy, Tejgarh, Gujarat, and particularly Prof Ganesh Devy, for generously hosting in February, 2008, a two-day workshop of members of the EC and authors to review the draft reports. We thank the members of the Advisory Board of the SAIP, who with their participation in the first consultation and later whenever called upon, gave their inputs to the reports. Thanks are due to Shankar Gopalakrishnan who meticulously put together statistical data and selected literature for SAIP.

Finally we would like to acknowledge and thank our funders ICCO, Netherlands, and TROCAIRE, Ireland, who supported the programme right through the last five years. We are grateful to the Foundation for Ecological Security, Anand, Gujarat, who generously supported the printing of the first phase of reports on land. We thank all of them for being patient with this initiative.

December, 2010

E Deenadayalan
General Secretary

Contents

Abbreviations Glossary

ALT	Agricultural Land Tribunal
BTAL	Bombay Tenancy and Agricultural Lands Act 1948
EGS	Employment Guarantee Scheme
ITDP	Integrated Tribal Development Project
MLRC	Maharashtra Land Revenue Code
MRT	Maharashtra Revenue Tribunal
NA	Non-agricultural (N.A.)
NP	National Park
NGO	Non-Government Organisation
PGA	Professional Golfers' Association
PHC	Primary Health Centre
SDO	Sub Divisional Officer
ST	Scheduled Tribes
TILR	Taluka Inspector of Land Records
WLS	Wild Life Sanctuaries

Preface

Eighty-eight million Adivasis and indigenous peoples live in India – approximately one fourth of the world's total indigenous population. Historically self-sufficient, forest-based communities with independent cultural identities, they have been subjected to displacement, dispossession and repression for more than a century and are now India's poorest and most marginalised communities. Since the onset of British rule, and in many cases from much earlier, Adivasis and indigenous peoples have been systematically and forcibly dispossessed of the resources of their homelands. In gross violation of democratic practice, social justice and both constitutional and legal requirements, such dispossession continues to this day. It is also the Adivasis and indigenous peoples who have paid the heaviest price for the current neo-liberal globalisation policies, with their land, resources and forests taken from them for private capital - in the name of 'economic growth.'

These larger processes have been accompanied by the erosion and undermining of cultural identities, leading to a loss of cultural moorings and other markers of ethnicity. Less than half of India's Adivasi communities speak their own language. State and private efforts at 'mainstreaming' and against indigenous faiths, practices and cultural mores have had a devastating impact.

Such trends have not gone unchallenged. Despite growing differentiation, ethnicity has emerged as a strong, consolidating force. Many have organised, often with the help of sympathetic outsiders, to fight against their oppressors and struggle for the control over land and other resources, and for local self-government as in parts of Central India. There have been demands for political self-determination and autonomy of varying degrees as in Jharkhand and the north-east. The state characterises all such struggles as 'Law and Order Problems', and large parts of central India and the north-east are heavily militarised in the name of 'national security'. In other parts too state repression has been heavy and brutal.

Though these processes are well known to many and particularly to Adivasis and indigenous people's movements, there continues to be a dearth of knowledge on the overall status of Adivasis and indigenous peoples in India. The struggle-based mass organisations of Adivasis and indigenous peoples in the Indian subcontinent articulated the need to work towards such a task in the late 1990s. The collective process to fulfil this task was launched in 2005.

The Status of Adivasis/Indigenous Peoples is conceptualised as a series of reports on salient themes affecting the lives of Adivasis/Indigenous Peoples. In the first instance, the series focuses on the situation of land and mining in the tribal tracts of the country. We hope that the series will be effective in not only deliberating upon similar themes of importance to the Adivasi present and future, but also help strengthening linkages amongst movements, activists, scholars and all others who are concerned with the protection of the rights of Adivasis/Indigenous Peoples in the Indian subcontinent.

This series of reports will explore the history, the laws, and the facts, and describe struggles while providing an overview of current realities. The main purpose of these reports is to expand linkages and relationships between movements, scholars, and activists so that the future of the political struggles is informed and forward looking.

Executive Summary

Only 57% of tribals in Maharashtra own land. However, the continuous onslaught by capital is slowly but surely eating into this survival base of the adivasis. This is due to the high rate of urbanisation and industrialization, increasing tourism and farmhouse culture on the one hand and displacement due to projects on the other. Land Reform legislations had the opposite effect to what was intended. Even the Restoration Acts have had very meager success. There appears to be a trend towards the withdrawal of the protective legislations. Infrastructure development for SEZs is leading to tribal land alienation in the hinterland.

The forests hold the key to the future of the adivasi areas. The proper implementation of the Scheduled Tribes and Other Forest Dwellers (Recognition of Forest Rights) Act 2006 will ensure recognition of hitherto unrecorded rights. However, take-over of forests must be concomitant with recognition of cultivation rights on forest land, if the real land issue in adivasi areas i.e. Self-rule of adivasi homelands – is to be properly addressed.

The increasing stratification of adivasi communities is leading to a breakdown of traditional communitarian ties and attachment to land. The emerging elite within the community is trying to consolidate its landholdings. In the absence of strong progressive peoples' movements the decimation of adivasi communities is a fait accompli. Even where strong peoples' movements exist, the dice is so loaded that the future looks very uncertain.

1

Introduction

The state of Maharashtra has the second largest tribal population in the country next only to that of Madhya Pradesh. The tribal peoples number 85.77 lakhs and constitute 8.9% of the state's population (2001). The major tribal communities are the Bhils, Gonds, Mahadev Kolis, Warlis, Koknas and Thakars, while the Katkaris, Kolam and Madia Gonds are classified as primitive tribes. Of the 47 Scheduled Tribes (ST) communities, 19 ST communities have a population of less than 1,000. The major tribal communities and their geographical location is given in Table 1[1].

TABLE 1: Major Tribal Communities in Maharashtra Showing Geographic Location

Name of tribe	*Total population (in lakhs)*	*% of tribal population*	*District wise geographic location*
Bhil	18.18	21.2	Nandurbar, Dhule, Nashik
Gond	15.54	18.1	Gadchiroli, Chandrapur, Wardha, Nagpur, Bhandara, Gondia, Yavatmal
Mahadev Koli	12.28	14.3	Ahmednagar, Thane, Nashik, Buldhana
Warli	6.27	7.3	Thane, Nashik, Mumbai
Kokna	5.72	6.7	Thane, Nashik
Thakar	4.88	5.7	Raigad, Thane, Nashik

1. Census of India 2001

STs are found in every district of the State, but six districts (Thane, Nashik, Nandurbar, Yavatmal, Nagpur and Dhule) account for 54% of the tribal population.[2] Major concentrations are in the western hilly Sahayadri region (Nandurbar, Dhule, Nashik, Thane and Raigad districts); and the Satpuda and Mahadeo hill ranges in central Gondwana (Gadchiroli, Chandrapur, Bhandara, Nagpur, Amravati and Yavatmal districts). The district-wise distribution of the major concentrations is given in Table 2[3]. Nandurabar has the highest concentration of Scheduled tribes, while Thane district boasts of the highest ST population.

TABLE 2: District wise distribution of STs in Maharashtra

District	*ST population of total district (lakhs)*	*ST as %age of total district population*	*No. of Blocks scheduled*
1. Nandurbar	8.59	65.53	5
2. Gadchiroli	3.72	38.31	8
3. Dhule	4.44	25.97	3
4. Nashik	11.94	23.92	7
5. Yavatmal	4.73	19.26	4
6. Chandrapur	3.75	18.12	1
7. Gondia	1.96	16.36	Nil
8. Thane	11.99	14.75	10
9. Amravati	3.56	13.68	2
10. Wardha	1.54	12.49	Nil
11. Raigad	2.69	12.19	Nil
12. Jalgaon	4.35	11.84	3
13. Nagpur	4.44	10.93	Nil

Nearly 96% of the tribal people live in the rural areas and constitute the poorest section of society. High infant mortality, pervasive malnutrition of women and children, malnutrition induced infant mortality, which are all indicators

2. ibid
3. Prabhu, Pradip. *Legally looted and cheated – Land reforms and Tribals in Maharashtra,* 2007a.

of high poverty levels, have been widespread for generations. However, the enormity of this human catastrophe found place in the media only in the past ten to fifteen years. What is a cause for alarm is that malnutrition and malnutrition induced deaths are not confined only to the inaccessible and backward areas, but occur with unfailing regularity even in Thane district, adjacent to the political, financial and industrial capital, Mumbai. The vast chasm that separates the tribals from the rest of the population of a state, which boasts of being one of the most advanced industrialized states of the country, is the cumulative result of land alienation, loss of forest habitat and displacement. These three factors that define the Adivasi situation and which individually and conjointly lead to rapid impoverishment, continue to pose grave questions about the role of land reforms in the tribal areas of Maharashtra.[4]

4. ibid

2

Adivasi Land Resources – A Macro View

Over 90% of male and 94% of female tribal workers are engaged in cultivation and land related activities[5]. Out of the 94.7 lakh operational land holdings extending over 209.24 lakh ha all over the state, 6.34 lakh operational holdings are those of the Adivasis covering 15.32 lakh ha. Tribal land holdings, therefore, are 6.7% of the total accounting for 7.3% of the land. Of these, 5.77 lakh holdings covering 15.37 lakh ha are individual holdings while 0.57 lakh holdings covering 1.75 lakh ha are collective holdings.[6]

2.1 Landholding pattern and Size of landholdings

The overall landlessness of tribals in Maharashtra is 43%. However, the regional disparities are tremendous as can be seen from Table 3[7] below.

More than 60% of the tribals in the ITDP Areas of Pen (Raigad district), Yawal (Jalgaon district), Shahapur (Thane district) and Pandharkawda (Yavatmal district) are landless. However landlessness is comparatively much lower (less than 30%) in the ITDP areas of Gadchiroli and Bhamragad (Gadchiroli district) and Ghodegaon (Ahmednagar district) and Rajura (Chandrapur district). Shahapur is an area where

5. Census of India, 2001.
6. Prabhu, Pradip, 2007a, op. cit.
7. Government of Maharashtra, Tribal Research and Training Institute, Adapted from Bench Mark Survey data.

TABLE 3: Land holding pattern of STs in Maharashtra (in %age)

ITDP area	*Land-less*	*Less than 1ha.*	*1-2 ha.*	*2-3 ha.*	*3-5 ha.*	*5-10 ha.*	*Greater than 10 ha*
Pen	68	7.36	14.40	4.48	3.84	1.60	0.32
Yawal	66	11.90	11.90	4.42	4.42	1.36	0.00
Shahapur	63	14.80	15.17	4.07	2.22	0.74	0.00
Pandharkawda	62	2.60	18.24	5.70	6.84	3.80	0.76
Taloda	56	12.76	18.92	5.72	3.96	1.76	0.00
Akola	51	10.78	22.54	7.35	5.88	1.96	0.49
Nagpur	51	10.29	22.54	7.84	5.88	1.96	0.49
Chimur	50	20.00	19.00	5.00	4.50	1.50	0.00
Nandurbar	47	13.25	23.85	8.48	5.83	2.12	0.00
Kinwat	45	10.45	27.50	7.70	6.60	2.20	0.00
Jawhar	44	14.00	24.08	9.52	5.60	2.24	0.00
Chandrapur	43	13.11	25.65	7.98	6.84	2.85	0.57
Dharni	43	7.41	23.94	8.55	10.83	5.70	0.57
Aheri	38	17.98	26.04	8.68	6.82	1.86	0.00
Nashik	38	18.60	22.32	9.92	7.44	3.10	0.62
Dahanu	36	30.72	24.96	6.40	1.92	00	0.00
Kalwan	32	20.40	25.84	10.88	7.48	2.72	0.68
Deori	32	26.52	26.52	8.16	5.44	1.36	0.00
Gadchiroli	28	20.88	30.24	10.08	7.92	2.16	0.72
Bhamragad	18	14.76	35.26	13.94	13.12	4.10	0.82
Ghodegaon	15	18.70	30.60	16.15	11.90	5.95	0.85
Rajur	12	17.60	33.44	17.60	13.20	5.28	0.88
Total	42.6	15.2	23.8	8.6	6.7	2.6	0.4

peasant castes co-exist with Adivasis. The Katkaris of Pen have moved directly from being forest dwelling food gatherers to becoming labourers in the unorganized sector, and as such have never owned much land. Both Shahapur and Pen are situated in close proximity to the industrialised and urban hubs of Thane and Navi Mumbai. All these factors have contributed to severe landlessness. On the other hand, the relative inaccessibility and remoteness of Gadchiroli district has provided some 'protection' to Adivasis and their lands.

Amongst tribes, landlessness is highest among the

Primitive Tribal Group of Katkaris (83%) and Kolams (63%). However, the other Primitive Tribal Group of Madia Gonds is mainly landed, with only 17% of them being landless. This is reflected in the ITDP area wise data in Table 3. Pen area (63% landlessness) is mainly inhabited by Katkaris, while Madia Gonds are to be found in Gadchiroli district (18-28% landlessness). In Raigad district, 57.82% of Katkaris were found to be landless.[8] However, 21.45% were *Dali* plot holders, i.e. cultivating land that had been leased to them by the forest department in the late 1890s. Interestingly, 'encroachments' on forest land were a negligible 0.67%. This is reflective of the fact that while the other more powerful Adivasi groups are able to negotiate the lower level forest officials, the Katkaris are unable to do so.

As mentioned earlier, the land holding pattern is closely related to the phenomenon of malnutrition and malnutrition related deaths in the Adivasi areas. In Nandurbar district, '72% of families (in which malnutrition related deaths had occurred) owned less than 3 acres, of which 40% were landless or owned less than one acre.'.[9] Further, 88% of families in which malnutrition related deaths occurred were landless.

The majority of Adivasis own poor quality land. Those who live in the hilly areas cultivate the coarser millets (*nagli, vari* etc.), whose yields are low. In many areas, the lands are left fallow in rotation cycles. Thus the data on size of landholdings does not reflect the actual area under cultivation. Further, an over-whelming majority (85.8%) of the land held by tribals is un-irrigated.[10] This is especially so

8. Sathe Vijay and Ghevde Bansi. *Study of Katkaris in Karjat taluka in Aug-Oct 2002 in Katkari, Academy of Development Studies,* 2003.
9. Government of Maharshtra. *Malnutrition related deaths of Tribal Children in Nandurbar district,* Tribal Research and Training Institute, 2002.
10. Government of India. *Report on Agricultural census 1990-91,* Department of Agriculture and Co-operation, Ministry of Agriculture.

in Thane district (Dahanu (1.0%), Jawhar (1.4%), Shahapur (1.44%) and Raigad district (Pen (2.0%).[11] Irrigated landholders constitute 4.3% of the tribal households in the state, while 8.6% have both irrigated and un-irrigated lands.[12]

As mentioned above, most of the land is individually owned. However a total of 1.75 lakh ha of land is shown to be collectively owned. Sacred groves are found in the Adivasi areas of Vidarbha and in the mountainous passes from the sea coast to the Sahyadris. Gadgil and Vartak estimated 250, while Deshmukh enumerated 383 such groves. 49% of the groves are on Revenue land, 12% on Forest land, 32% on privately owned land and 7% are on temple trust land. The size of such groves varies from a clump of trees to an area expanding over 60 ha, with an average size of 1.5 ha. The burial ground groves or *masutias* (eg. Bhairoba sacred grove) found in Mahadeo Koli and Kunbi villages, may be owned by the village, hamlet, clans, castes or individuals.[13]

Shifting cultivation was, by and large, wiped out in the last decades of the 19th century, when the Adivasis were evicted from forest land. However, shifting cultivation continues to be practiced by Madia Gonds in about 11-12 villages in the dense forests of Bhamragad. They cultivate small patches adjacent to their settled plots.[14]

It is to be noted that the data on landholdings available is about the legal land-holdings on revenue land. It does not reflect the lands that are being cultivated by Adivasis under lease (*Ek-Sali* and *Dali*), nor does it reflect the cultivation in forests that the government refers to as 'encroached plots'.

---

11. Government of Maharashtra, Tribal Research and Training Institute, Adapted from Bench Mark Survey data.
12. Government of India. *Report on Agricultural census 1990-91*, Department of Agriculture and Co-operation, Ministry of Agriculture.
13. Burman, Roy JJ. *Sacred Groves Among Communities*, Mittal Publications, 2003.
14. Interview with Rucha Ghate, Nagpur, May 2007.

There are also fairly large tracts of government wastelands that are being cultivated by Adivasis and others.

2.2 Land – What it means: Then and Now

In Maharashtra, as in most other Adivasi areas, land and forests belonged to the Adivasi communities till the beginning of the last century. Government records of the time indicate that at the beginning of the previous century, the pattern of land ownership was invariably one wherein land belonged to the community, and was administered by the village elders with usufructary rights with the separate families. This traditional land holding system, in which the individual rights of enjoyment of land and land-based resources were enmeshed in communal systems of access to and management of resources, was fundamentally different from mere allocation of land *pattas* to individual families. It was the basis of the polity, economy and culture of the Adivasis. The notion of ownership was radically different. There existed no concept of 'exclusive title' or 'exclusive possession' as a private domain of the individual against the rest of the community. Ownership was best understood as 'mutual respect and recognition of the access of an individual or family' to a separate plot of land to be utilized for the 'special requirements' of the family. It provided for 'particularities of individual requirements' within the 'generality of the communal cultivation'. When *jhum*[15] was suppressed, the 'separate plot' concept extended to the land being accessed by an individual in the intervening period till land settlements began.[16]

On the 'individually accessed plots', however, all naturally growing fruit trees belonged to the village, which meant that all the residents of the village could access those trees, or the concerned family would share the fruits of the

15. Called also as slash and burn or shifting cultivation.
16. Prabhu, Pradip, 2007a., op. cit.

tree with the whole village. There was therefore no notion of private ownership in the consciousness of the tribal people. Land did not and could not belong to the individual (as a commodity that could be bought, sold, transferred or mortgaged or alienated in any other manner), but the individual belonged to land (as habitat, history, geography and territory) by virtue of his ancestors being seated in the given territory. Land, circumscribed the individuals' and community's existence as an extension of their collective consciousness. Land had not merely an economic significance as a survival resource, it had also a social (the basis of a person's sense of belonging to a specific cultural community), cultural (the link to traditions, ethos and way of life) and political significance (the material basis for the power of the elders to manage the community). Thus, land and forests in the 'present time' are the means through which the community hands over its past (history, culture, ethos, traditions) to the future generations. Land is the vital 'permanent' link between 'transient' generations of human beings and thereby an embodiment of consciousness. Loss of land, i.e. the transfer of resources or the mere change in the land use pattern, whatever the scale of such change, is by itself not alienation, it is the 'material basis' for alienation. The individual or community are uprooted from the concrete articulation of their consciousness and are progressively pushed into anomie. The criticality of land alienation in the life and psyche of the tribal people therefore can never be under-estimated.[17] As land was community owned, the question of individual titles did not exist. However today, while the community feeling does exist in Adivasi societies, it does not extend to landholdings. The consciousness of the peasant has become entrenched in the Adivasi's mind. Disputes over boundaries abound in every village. Many who are educated try and exploit the discrepancies in the land records to their benefit fuelling internal conflicts. The Adivasi

17. Prabhu, Pradip, 2007a., op. cit.

wishes to have exclusive title to land and thus the issue of *'khate phod'* (or partition of lands) has become important to him.

Land has also begun to be viewed as a commodity that can be bought and sold. Those Adivasis who live in close proximity to the towns prefer to sell their lands. They view the statutes that provide protection to their lands as impediments to earning some quick money. In practical terms when builders invest crores in high rise buildings that come up on all sides of a tribal landholding, the tribal finds it profitable to sell his land. Of course, that he gets a poor deal in the bargain is a different story.

The Adivasis had been practicing shifting agriculture prior to the entry of the British. Even so, the Warli tribal story of Kanseri, talks of how the men-folk, symbolized by *Mirig* (the god of Rain), are ignorant of agricultural practices, unlike the women, symbolized by *Kanseri* (the goddess of grain).[18] However, ironically, when revenue land settlements were made in the late 1880s, such titles were made in the names of the males. There are also other indications that women continued to play a more important role in many of Adivasi societies till as recently as the late nineteenth century. It is interesting to note that the decline in their status corresponds to the period when land titles were granted to men.

Today, as per revenue law, women are to be treated at par with men and the name of the female heir is to be recorded along with that of the male heirs in the land records. However, often her name gets relegated to the 'other rights' column. And in innumerable cases, her name just does not appear anywhere in the records. The rights of widows are of special significance. If she prefers to live independently with her children in her marital or natal home, she is almost never allowed independent access to the family land. If she remarries, she must leave her children behind if they are to

18. Prabhu, Pradip, 2007a., op. cit.

inherit the family property. If a mother insists on child custody, it means the loss of all rights over paternal property. Although customary law provides for inheritance by male children, in practice this results in bitter, expensive, and wasteful, legal battles over property with paternal relatives. It is not uncommon for a widow/single woman to be accused of being a witch by her own sons or brothers-in-law if she dares to assert her control over the family property.[19]

19. Bulsara, Shiraz. *The Rights of Single Tribal Women*, unpublished paper.

3

A Historical Tracing of the Pattern of Tribal Land Alienation

3.1 Eviction from Forests, Land Settlements and Land Seizures

The seizure of Adivasi homelands and their conversion into Reserved and Protected forests took place in all Adivasi areas of the state. In Thane district 'by a notification, nearly 401,566 acres of free grazing land was included into forest of one or another description'.[20] The land thus acquired amounted to nearly 50% of the forest area of the District. 30% of the lands originally classified as wasteland, not privately owned, mostly in small tracts of semi-forested lands, controlled by the villagers through their elders, belonging to the Adivasis, were taken away from them overnight and merged into the forest. In a short span of 32 years after the area was ceded to the British in 1818, the administration brutally suppressed the practice of shifting cultivation practiced by Adivasis and forced them out from the forest and resettled them in more or less permanent habitations on the fringes of the forest.[21]

By virtue of the Land Settlement of 1856, the Adivasis were granted alienable title to land. They were required to pay revenue in cash to the British. Land, which till then was not privately owned, became a commodity that could be

20. *Report of the Bombay Forest Commission*, 1887.
21. ibid

bought and sold, transferred and alienated. Interestingly, Section 73 of The Bombay Land Revenue Code (Act 5 of 1879) specifically recognized the right to sell, mortgage, bequeath or otherwise to transfer land.

This heralded the process of alienation to the following categories of persons:

(a) the local land holding peasant castes in the *ryotwari*[22] areas like the Agris or Kunbis in Thane and Raigarh or the Gujjars in Dhule, the latter who moved into the Adivasi areas in search of land after the areas were opened up by the British.

(b) non-cultivating but landed gentry also in the *ryotwari* areas, like the Maldharis in Chandrapur and Gadchiroli districts or the Khots in Raigarh.

(c) non-cultivating non-peasant castes, largely traders, merchants and contractors in most parts of the *ryotwari* areas, who entered the Adivasis areas as shop-keepers, traders, timber contractors, alcohol vendors through the mediation of the colonial administration.

(d) non-cultivating, non-peasant castes, largely members of the lower nobility, officials in the army eg. *inamdars, izzafatdars, zamindars* and *faznadeiros*, who were granted large tracts through the mediation of the pre-colonial rulers.[23]

In Thane district, outsiders, viz. Marwaris, Vanias, Parsis and Muslims entered the area as moneylenders, shopkeepers, liquor contractors and timber contractors. The American Civil War led to an export of cotton and cotton cultivation spread in Dhule and Nasik districts. The Superintendent, Deccan and Gujarat Revenue Surveys, writing in 1864, ten years after his first visit to Shahada taluka in Dhulia district states,

---

22. A system used to collect revenues from the cultivators of agricultural land.
23. Prabhu, Pradip, 2007a., op. cit.

'.....Pasture land has given way to cultivation, more than half of which is producing exportable crops. .....the increase in the Gujar population is worth noting. It seems to me that the taluka is destined to be populated by people from Gujarat.' With the development of transport facilities, establishment of peaceful conditions and commercialization of agriculture, non-Adivasi agriculturists began to move into areas inhabited by Adivasis. The movement was particularly marked in areas like Shahada, Taloda, and Nandurbar taluka in Dhule district.[24]

The Adivasis became increasingly victims of exploitation, falling into debt, as they had no knowledge or experience of the monetary system. They were required to pay the revenue to the State in cash as stipulated by the settlement, and were illiterate, hence unaware what documents their thumb impressions were taken on.

This period also corresponded with the establishment of the judicial system, which is based on the presumed veracity of documentary evidence and adversarial jurisprudence. The Adivasi was unable to cope with the alien legal system and an alien language. The legal system, almost blindly, gave legal sanction for the patently illegal appropriation of land from the Adivasis, contributed to its commodification and legitimized the debt trap.

As a result of the processes set in motion after Thane district was ceded to the British, notwithstanding the two land settlements of 1890 and 1920, the majority of the Adivasis, particularly the Warlis were reduced to tenants, bonded or forced labourers and marriage serfs on what was once their own land; their masters being the Marwaris, Parsis, Vanis and Muslims.

Later on, the Government of Bombay recognized the extent and undesirability of such large scale alienation and in 1901, amended Section 73 of the Bombay Land Revenue

24. Kulkarni, Sharad. *Alienation and Restoration of Adivasis' lands in Maharashtra*, NCAS publication.

Code that validated land transfers (Act 6 of 1901). Under this amendment, the Government was empowered to make certain lands non-transferable without the previous sanction of the Collector. From time to time, this power was used to declare lands in certain Adivasi inhabited areas as non-transferable without the Collector's previous sanction. However, not all the Adivasi inhabited areas were covered under this section. Moreover, despite the restrictions, transfers continued unabatedly, as the Collectors gave their sanction to transfers quite freely. The result was that by 1938, Adivasis of Shahada who constituted 31.7% of the population owned just 5.3% of the land. Similarly in Thane district, the Adivasis despite being 47% of the population held only 4.1% of the lands.[25] Similar figures are available for Kalwan taluka of Nashik district.

While the experience of the Adivasis of Melghat (Amravati district) is very similar, the story in Chandrapur district is slightly different. This is because of the existence of Adivasi kings (Gond rajas) at Nagpur (Devgiri), Chandrapur (Ballarpur), and in Gadmandla (Madhya Pradesh). Further, as mentioned earlier, being more remote, the tentacles of the outsiders were not able to penetrate the Adivasi areas of Gadchiroli as much as in Thane and Raigad districts.

3.2 Urbanisation and Industrialisation

In Mumbai, the expansion of the city, especially to provide infrastructure, resulted in entire Adivasi hamlets being wiped off the face of the earth. There are 72 Adivasi hamlets and 152 Adivasi slum-settlements inhabited by about 1.5 to 2 lakh Adivasis within Greater Mumbai.[26] Numerous Adivasi

25. Symington, D. *Report on the Aboriginal and Hill Tribes of the partially excluded areas in Bombay Presidency*, 1938.
26. Maharshtra Shasan, Adivasi Vikas Vibhag , Tribal Research and Training Institute :Brihanmumbai Mahanagti va Mumbai Upanagar Zilhyatel Padyanche sarvekshan avahal , 2005.

hamlets in northern Mumbai have disappeared into the Sahar Airport, the Aarey Milk Colony and the Sanjay Gandhi National Park at Borivali. When the Wadia Trust handed over 760 acres to the administration for setting up the Aarey Milk Colony, there were 21 Adivasi hamlets existing on the land. Initially, the administration leased out land to a few Adivasis at Re. 1/- per *guntha*[27], but later the Adivasis were evicted from these lands. In 1965 the Aarey Colony gave over land to the Veterinary College. In 1972, two Adivasi *padas*[28] – Bhurikhanpada and Khadakpada were to be evicted to make way for Picnic Point and picnic gardens. But Adivasis organized an *andolan*[29] under leadership of Nanasaheb Gore, resulting in the protection of some lands. Similarly Modern Bakeries has come up on what were originally Adivasi lands. Devipada and Habalpa da were handed over to the Film City to set up a 400 acre complex. Of these in 2001, 25 acres were handed over to Subhash Ghai to set up 'Whistling Woods' Training Centre. Subhash Ghai, with the help of police, bulldozed the houses of Adivasis on 28 January 2002. Adivasi lands were also taken over for the setting up of the Mahananda Dairy.[30]

The people of Mumbai require not only milk for sustenance and films for entertainment but also a National Park for recreation. The Sanjay Gandhi National Park at Borivali is inhabited by many, many more Adivasis than tigers. The 1991 Census indicated that there were 970 families in the Borivali National Park. Yet, in 1993 the Park authorities, municipality and police destroyed huts along the border of the Park. The Deputy Conservator of forests noted in his affidavit that, 'The Adivasis were tilling lands owned by Aarey colony on 6 monthly lease for which they were paying

27. Guntha is a is a measure of area equal to 2.5 cents.
28. Hamlets.
29. Movement.
30. Patil, Nitin *Shapit*, Samarthan Publication, 2002.

taxes in kind to Aarey colony. Moreover, the Revenue authorities did not recognize the Adivasis staying in the Park as original inhabitants. They were just a *colony of migrants'*. Failing to recognize the difference between encroachments of slums and quarries within the National Park on the one hand, and the original Adivasi residents and farmers on the other, in 1997, the High Court passed a blanket order of eviction of all persons from the National Park.[26] Similarly, the urban sprawl of Nagpur city has extended on to what was once Adivasi lands. The adjacent Narkhed and Katol areas have also witnessed large scale land alienation. Every single market town in the Scheduled Area is teeming with non-tribals, including many government servants who live in houses that have illegally come up on Adivasi lands. Dharni town in Amravati is a glaring example.[27] While the law specifically prohibits the leasing out of Adivasi lands, except with the permission of the Collector, and that too for a maximum of five years, the phenomenon of 99-year leases is ubiquitous. No changes are effected in the land documents, but the possession of the land is transferred to the non-Adivasi. The juggernaut of industrialisation has also played havoc in Thane and Raigad districts. In Chandrapur, the Adivasis lost their lands to the Ambuja cement factory at Manikgad.[31]

3.3 Tourism

As Hill stations by definition come up on hilly land (where Adivasi live), the creation of new hill-stations must involve the alienation of Adivasi land. Most of these are coming up within a three hours' drive from Mumbai, such that the jet-set crowd from the metropolis can make a quick getaway. These new hill-stations are not like the quintessential Mahabaleshwar or Nainital, but are basically private resorts owned and developed by private companies. In some places,

31. Interview with Vijay Siddheshwar, Mul, Chandrapur, May 2007.

the developer sells houses and house- plots to private parties. The most famous of these hill-stations is Amby Valley that has come up in the Amby valley (formerly Ambewadi) in the Mulshi Lake area of Pune district. Constructed over rolling hills on an expanse of 10,000 acres, the resort which has been developed by the Sahara group boasts of a 7-star deluxe hotel, a private ropeway, an advanced communication centre, a shopping centre, an executive club, artificial lakes, fountains, artificial waterfalls etc. Nine-hundred luxury villas, timber chalets and Spanish cottages are being constructed. When completed Amby valley will boast of a private air-strip and a PGA[32] Golf course. Sahara group claims that Amby Valley is the 'most premium residential development in the country'.[33] Much of Amby valley was once Adivasi land. When a hue and cry was raised in the mid 1990s, the State government appointed the Varti committee to look into allegations. Instead of restoring the alienated land that had been illegally taken over, the government decided to issue new Special Regulations for development of tourist resorts/holiday homes/townships in hill station type areas on 26.11.1996. This set of regulations provides, inter alia, that the condition that only an agriculturist may buy agricultural land shall be waived in hill station-type areas, that the ceiling on agricultural land holdings would not apply to purchases made by the owners or developers of hill station projects, that agricultural land may be used for non-agricultural purposes without permission in an area declared a hill station and that hill station development would be treated as an industry.[34] Most importantly, Clause 17 of this Notification takes away the protection that section 36A of the Maharashtra Land Revenue Code provided to the tribal. In Section 36A, the Collector

32. Professional Golfers' Association
33. Padmanabhan, R, 1997-1998. *A Resort for the Rich* in Frontline, Vol. 14, No. 26, Dec 27 1997 – Jan 9 1998.
34. ibid.

had only discretionary powers to grant permission for transfer of Adivasi lands. Over the years, as the issue of transfer of Adivasi lands has become a sensitive issue, the Collectors have used these discretionary powers very sparingly. However, the new Notification states that the Collector *shall* grant permission to any person who wishes to acquire tribal land for the purpose of construction of a hill-station. The Collector is empowered to impose conditions, but he cannot refuse permission. Subsequently in 2005, the Bombay Tenancy and Agricultural Lands Act 1948 was amended to incorporate many of the provisions that had been covered in the Special Regulation.

Interestingly, this Regulation was issued on 26 November 1996, much after construction work had begun in the Amby valley. Even so, the transfer of land and subsequent construction was not declared to be illegal. Instead, Sahara group was asked to cough up a fine of Rs.5.5 million. This was peanuts for Sahara, which has till today invested more than Rs.45,000 million on the Project. The High Court passed a stay order on 23 June 1997, but subsequently the stay was lifted and construction was completed. Amby Valley – the home of the Mahadev Koli and Thakur tribals now plays host to business families, film stars, sportspersons and political bosses. Recently, it hosted the prestigious Laureus Sports Awards function and the Mrs. World Contest extravaganza.

Similar hill-stations have come up in Kamshet (Golden Glades) in Pune district. In Raigad district, the Mahalmirya Hill station was to come up in Pen taluka. In 1990 the plan was made public. Builders began buying land at Rs.7,500 per hectare from Adivasis and sold it at Rs.5-14 lakhs per hectare. In Sateri village, a builder began constructing a road through Adivasi private land. The *Shramik Kranti Sanghatna* stopped the construction of the same. All sales had taken place without permission of the Collector. A taluka level federation to oppose the illegal transfer of Adivasi lands and construction was formed. All transactions were stopped and

Mahalmirya Hill station remains a dream for the land sharks. However, in Tadgaon, where a similar hill-station, involving the construction of a 1,500 acre resort, with three dams and an amusement park, the mass organizations intervened late. By then, bungalows had already been constructed.[35] In recent years a large first of its kind township is coming up at Lavassa near Pune. Here too, irregularities in purchase of and illegal alienation of Adivasi lands abound.

3.4 Farmhouses

Similarly, the 'farmhouse culture' has spawned in the entire Adivasi area near Mumbai city. The urban elite and even the upper middle class purchase individual plots and construct private bungalows on the same. Some developers construct small cottages and sell them to the ever increasing buyers. As sale of tribal agricultural land is not permissible, the status of the land is first converted into non-agricultural and then sold. In cases where the land is not converted into non-agricultural (N.A.) category, the jet-set Mumbaikars dig up documents to show that their grandfathers or grandmothers are agriculturists owning land in some remote corner of the country. Such farmhouses have also come up in the Lohara and Ballarpur area of Chandrapur district. [36]

3.5 Displacement due to projects

The acquisition of Adivasi land in the name of development projects through the operation of the colonial Land Acquisition Act has pushed the Adivasis to the brink of survival, ruthlessly destroying the forest people through an all out attack on their basic right to live and work in the forest and is thus producing conditions bordering on ethnocide.[37]

The displacement of Adivasis in the Narmada Valley is

35. 31 Interview with Surekha Dalvi, Mumbai, January 2008
36. Interview with Vijay Siddheshwar, Mul, Chandrapur, May 2007.
37. Prabhu, Pradip, 2007a., op. cit.

well-known. Thirty three villages in Akrani taluka were submerged. The fact that they were forest villages, which have never been surveyed created insurmountable problems in rehabilitation. But the displacement due to smaller projects has often not received due attention. The scale of displacement in all these projects together is enormous. In many places, for minor irrigation projects, Adivasi land is being forcibly acquired by the authorities, without issuing notices under the Land Acquisition Act. In malnutrition endemic Amravati district, Adivasi lands have been submerged in the Sapan Nadi Project, Chandrabhaga Nadi Prakalp and Gopapur Dharan Prakalp[38] . In Mokhada taluka of Thane district, work began illegally on the Tulyachapada project and the Wagh Project in 1997 without following any of the provisions of the Land Acquisition Act. The Adivasis, under the banner of the *Kashtakari Sanghatna* stopped the work on the Wagh Project and obtained orders from the High Court to ensure that the provisions of the Land Acquisition Act were followed. Similar instances occurred in Igatpuri taluka of Nashik district.[39] In Rajura taluka of Chandrapur district, 350 acres of two Adivasi villages are in the submergence area of the Bhendara Irrigation Project. As no rehabilitation was planned, an NGO, *Shramik Elgar* stopped the work and approached the High Court who granted a stay on the Project, ruling 'first rehabilitation, then project'.[40]

But even where rehabilitation has taken place, much has been left to be desired.[41] In the Dimbhe Project, 57% of families did not receive alternative land prior to submergence. 20%

---

38. Interview with Bandya Sane, Paratwadi, Amravatai, May 2007.
39. Interview with Shiraz Bulsara, Dahanu, Thane, October 2007.
40. Interview with Vijay Siddheshwar, Mul, Chandrapur, May 2007.
41. Tribal Research and Training Institute, Government of Maharashtra. *Resettlement of Tribal Families Displaced by Irrigation Projects (Dimbhe and Pimpalgaon Joge Projects) in Pune district.*

of families who had paid the required amount for alternative land had not received the same. Despite receiving land in the command area, 54% of households had not received the benefits of irrigation. And overall there was a decrease of 55% in size of landholding post rehabilitation. It is interesting to note that in the Pimpalgaon Joge project fearing obstruction from the original holders at the resettlement site, the project displaced opted for subsidy/enhanced compensation instead of alternative land.[42] The Expressways that are being constructed to link the metros have bulldozed through the hills and Adivasi hamlets. Entire Katkari hamlets have made way for the Pune-Mumbai Highway. The widening of National Highway No. 8 linking Mumbai to Ahmedabad, goes right through the Scheduled Area. The land was never acquired either under the Land Acquisition Act or the National Highway Act, even when the Highway was first constructed in the 1950s. The Adivasi cultivators were never issued notices regarding the acquisition and did not receive compensation. In 2002-05 Adivasis under the banner of *Adivasi Punarvasan Andolan* forced the authorities to pay the compensation at market rates applicable for non-agricultural land for both previously illegally acquired lands and lands that are now being acquired. However all affected cultivators have till date not received compensation.[43] It is interesting to note that the Mumbai-Talasari Expressway which also goes through the Scheduled Area was stalled in 2000 on the grounds that the Gram Sabhas had not been consulted.[44]

There is also de facto acquisition of lands for roads, minor water bodies under Employment Guarantee Scheme (EGS), electric pylons for high tension cables etc.. It would be without exaggeration to state that virtually all the EGS roads

---

42. ibid.
43. Interview with SDO, Dahanu, Maya Patole, Dahanu, Thane , October 2008.
44. Interview with Shiraz Bulsara, Dahanu, Thane, October 2007.

in tribal districts have swallowed tribal lands without any legal acquisition or compensation for the tribal landholder. Similar is the case of minor water bodies like percolation tanks. For many government or zilla parishad run services like PHCs, Ashramshalas, land of Adivasis is being acquired without proper compensation (eg. Vasa PHC, Talasari taluka).

3.6 Mining

The Western Coalfields near Bhadravati (20 kms. From Chandrapur) acquired Adivasi lands resulting in the eviction of Adivasi families. Coal mines are situated at Padmapur and Nilzai, near Chandrapur. Similarly, Adivasis lost land at Murpaar near Chimur. Recently, the Adani group obtained permission to mine thousands of acres of land in the vicinity of the Tadoba Sanctuary.

4

Land Related Laws and Policies and their Consequences

4.1 Tenancy Legislation

The 1971 census figures of tribal land holdings, which correspond to 1961-1971 decadal conditions, are very revealing. The figures indicate that during the period immediately after the passage of the amended Bombay Tenancy and Agricultural Lands Act in 1957, the number of tribal cultivators, rather than increasing as a result of this important land reform legislation, actually fell from 7.25 lakhs in 1961 to 5.61 lakhs in 1971. The fall in the number of tribal cultivators by 1.64 lakhs in gross numbers leads to the alarming conclusion that precisely during the implementation of tenancy legislation, 22.62% of the tribals were rendered landless.[45] This systematic alienation of Adivasi lands may be segmented into two periods:

(a) Period between 1945 and 1 April 1957 (i.e. Tillers' Day - the day the Tenant was legally conferred with title)
(b) Post 1 April 1957

1940 to 1 April 1957:

Land reform was initiated in Mumbai Presidency by the Bombay Tenancy and Agricultural Lands Act 1939

45. Prabhu, Pradip, 2007a. op. cit.

promulgated during Home Rule, which created the category of 'protected tenants' who were granted protection from eviction. The Adivasis, in some areas, continued cultivating land that was rightfully theirs. However, once it became clear, that subsequent land reforms would restore land back to the Tiller, the landowners tried to scuttle the law in many ways:

(a) physical eviction of tenants and simultaneously deletion of their names from the land records, in collusion with the *Talathis* (*Patwaris*, the lowest revenue department officials).

(b) in collusion with the Tehsildars[46], landlords got the names of tenants legally deleted from the records as 'erroneously recorded', 'surrendered tenancies' or 'personal cultivation' or 'conversion of the tenant into wage labourer'. Innumerable non-tribal landlords 'forced' the tenants to 'voluntary surrender' their land to them under Section 15 of the Bombay Tenancy and Agricultural Lands (BTAL) Act, 1948. These 'voluntary surrenders' were not by any stretch of imagination voluntary, for it is near impossible to conceive that a tenant would voluntarily give away his land to a landlord. The land, instead, was physically appropriated. To prevent this from occurring, the BTAL Rules 1956, laid down in Rule 9, that 'The Mamlatdar,[47] when verifying the surrender of a tenancy by a tenant in favour of the landlord under Sec. 15, shall satisfy himself, after such enquiry as he thinks fit, that tenant understands the nature and consequences of the surrender and also that it is voluntary and shall endorse his findings in that behalf upon the instruments of surrender'. Such a provision for verification had also existed in the 1939 Act and Section 29 of the BTAL 1948 Act. But even so, in a

46. Revenue Administrative Officer of the Taluka
47. The chief revenue officer of a Taluka. same as the Tehsildar

case of 'voluntary surrender' the learned judge noted that, 'The Tahsildar did not verify that the surrender by the tribal was voluntary'. Further in another case,[42] the Sub-Divisional Officer had observed that 'the entry is in pencil which shows that the entry was not finally verified by the Tahsildar as required by the rules under the Record of Rights'. Most mutations under this provision were perfunctorily made. The Mutation Entries may make a mention of an order passed by the Tahsildar vide a Work Sheet (W.S), but copies of such W.S are never available for scrutiny.

(c) As no rent-receipts were ever issued by the landlords, they could easily claim that the tenants had not paid rent for three successive years and could thus terminate tenancy for 'Default of Tenant' under Sec. 14 of the BTAL Act. In Thane district alone, 1,190 cases of such type of 'default of tenant' have been recorded during the period 1950-51 to 1954-55.

The result of these machinations was that on 1 April 1957 many of the tenants' names were not present in the Record of Rights; they thus did not become deemed purchasers and were therefore summarily evicted following due process of law. In an official statement made in the Bombay Legislative Assembly on 19 March 1956, Mustafa Faki, on behalf of B.D.Hiray (then, Minister for Revenue and Agriculture), stated that in Thane District alone, 5,944 applications for securing possession of land from tenants were submitted during the period 1950-51 to 1954-55. (i.e. prior to the 1957 Act) and that 1,592 of these applications, led to official evictions.[48]

Post 1 April 1957:

Those landlords who were not successful in evicting tenants during the 12 years post the 1948 Tenancy Act, repeated the

48. Prabhu, Pradip, 2007a, op. cit.

same stratagems during the Sec.32 G proceedings under the Tenancy Act (i.e. proceedings to determine the purchase price to be paid by the tenant for the land the landlords) in conjunction with the Agricultural Land Tribunal (ALT) which conducted the proceedings. The following methods were adopted:

(a) Through the collusion with the *Talathis*, many landlords were successful in getting the tenants to put thumb impressions on applications stating that they were not tenants in possession on 1.4.57, and therefore were not deemed purchasers.

(b) Some landlords managed to con Adivasis into signing similar declarations before the ALT or to declare that they were not interested in purchasing the land and it could therefore revert back to the landlord. The tenant was made out to be 'unwilling to purchase the land'.[49] In the former case, the Maharashtra Revenue Tribunal (MRT), while restoring the land to the tribal, remarked that a purchase cannot be made ineffective by the landlord just stating that the tribal was unwilling to purchase the land. Yet thousands of such cases occurred.

(c) In some instances, during Section 32G proceedings the tenant was shown as 'servant' and thus could not be termed as 'deemed purchaser' and therefore forfeited his right to purchase the land.[50]

(d) When the purchase price was fixed, it was fixed for an area less than that originally held by the tribal tenant.[51]

---

49. Court Records. Maharashtra Revenue Tribunal, Mumbai, Case No 175/78, and Sub-divisional Magistrate, Dahanu, Case No. 180/3 of 1978, Heard and disposed of.
50. Court Records. Maharashtra Revenue Tribunal, Mumbai, Case No 77/80, Heard and disposed of.
51. Court Records. Maharashtra Revenue Tribunal, Mumbai, Case No 58/80, Heard and disposed of.

(e) No proceedings had taken place under Section 32 G at all. Instead the Tahsildar had just ordered that the tenants' names to be deleted under sections 14, 29 and 31 of the Tenancy Act, i.e. default of rent and exemption for personal cultivation by landlord.[52]

Other than subversion of Section 32 Proceedings, the following methods were adopted:

(a) Forgery of records: One important judgement says, '...the ink is also different in colour ... the entry is suspicious'.[53]

(b) Deceit: Another judgement reads as follows, '... she (non-tribal) has been practicing deceit on him; obtained his thumb impression and deprived him of his land ...... took away his land from him by telling him that she would give him some other land; but that she never done so'.[54]

The above is corroborated by a Study conducted by Probationers of the Indian Administrative Service in 1994.[55]

Further a recent study shows that an overwhelming majority (72%) of the tribal occupants who have lost possession and title to their lands were legal owners of the land on Tillers Day i.e. 1 April 1957. These legal owners were divested of their rights and illegally evicted, notwithstanding the fact that their status was recorded.[56] The following table

52. Court Records. Maharashtra Revenue Tribunal, Mumbai, Case Nos. 123/77; 124/77; 125/77; 126/77; 127/77; 102/77; 103/77; 104/77; 157/77; 158/77; 165/77; Heard and disposed of.
53. Court Records. Maharashtra Revenue Tribunal, Mumbai, Case No 109/80, Heard and disposed of.
54. Court Records. Maharashtra Revenue Tribunal, Mumbai, Case No 172/78, Heard and disposed of.
55. Lal Bahadur Shastri National Academy of Administration, 1994. *Land Reforms in India: An Empirical Study*, Land Reform Unit, Mussoorie.
56. Prabhu, Pradip, 2007b. *Tribal Land Alienation in Thane district* (unpublished).

from the said study in Thane district shows the methods employed to alienate the lands:

TABLE 4: Means by Which Tribal Land was Alienated[57]

How Title Alienated	*Shahapur taluka*	*Dahanu Taluka*	*Total*
Legally – Tenancy Deleted	6	3	9
Legally – Tenancy Surrendered	2	0	2
Legally – Wrong Entry	2	0	2
Tenancy Deleted – Evacuee Land	1	0	1
Illegally – Tenancy Deleted	21	27	48
Illegally – Evicted	13	8	21
Unrecorded Tenancy	3	10	13
Acquired – Private Forest	2	0	2
Land Consolidation	0	2	2
	50	50	100

Land reforms resulted in wave upon wave of initiatives of the landed elite to extinguish rights and eradicate documentary evidence, which could have resulted in ownership for the tenant. The very law that intended to convert the 'tenant at will', provided the impetus for increasing numbers of 'tenants at will' to become invisible in law.

Restrictions were imposed in 1966 on the transfer of tribal lands by the Maharashtra Land Revenue Code (Section 36 A) to curb this malpractice and they came into effect in August 1967. Notwithstanding the prohibitions, the Collectors and Deputy Commissioners routinely granted permission.

The result was that widespread alienation of tribal lands continued unabated. In 1972, a Committee appointed by the *Maharashtra Sarvodaya Mandal* found that in 57 villages in Shahada taluka of Dhule district, about 10,000 acres of land was transferred to non-Adivasis. Dhule District Co-operative Bank made a survey of 10 villages and found that about 2,000

57. ibid.

acres of land had been alienated. The Committee appointed to inquire into the land problems of Adivasis by the Government of Maharashtra noted that it found 28 cases in Nandurbar taluka of Dhule district alone, of land being leased in by non-Adivasis and later on purchased by them under the provisions of the Tenancy Act ![58]

4.2 The Restoration Acts

Demands to prohibit transfers of lands held by Adivasis to non-Adivasis were made from time to time by several social workers working among the Adivasis and political parties. *Morchas*[59] and demonstrations took place. *Andolans* in Palghar taluka of Thane district by the *Bhoomi Sena* and in Dhule district by the *Shramik Sanghatna*, forced the government to take note of the alarming situation. The demand also found its echo in the State legislature. In the winter session of the Bombay Legislature of 1970, an Adivasi member moved a non-official bill to amend the Maharashtra Land Revenue Code. The Bill was withdrawn after an assurance was given by the Government that it would appoint a committee to inquire into the problem. Accordingly, the Committee to 'Examine Difficulties Experienced by Scheduled Tribe Land Holders/Cultivators in Respect of Their Lands in the Working of Certain Acts' was appointed in March 1971 under the chairmanship of the then Revenue Minister H.G. Vartak. The Committee submitted its Report in April 1972.[60] It observed that the ban on the permissions for transfer of lands was being flouted by Collectors freely and now they themselves were being required to declare the earlier orders of these officials as illegal.[61] This was unrealistic. The Committee made several recommendations to restrict the

---

58. Kulkarni, Sharad, op cit.
59. Protest rallies.
60. Kulkarni, Sharad, op cit.
61. Kulkarni, Sharad, op cit.

future transfer of lands held by Adivasis and to restore the lands already transferred.

The Government accepted the recommendations of the Committee and on 6 July 1974 it issued an ordinance to prohibit the transfer of lands held by Adivasis to non-Adivasis and to restore lands transferred in contravention of legal provisions (Maharashtra Ordinance 13 of 1974). Later, this was converted into the Maharashtra Land Revenue Code and Tenancy Laws (Amendment) Act 1974, also called Act no. 35 of 74.

Some of the main provisions of this Act are as follows:

(a) No transfer of Adivasi lands to non-Adivasis is permitted except with permission of the Collector, and that too where the transfer is by way of lease or mortgage not exceeding five years.

(b) In other cases, prior permission of State Government is necessary before granting permission to transfer, sell, or exchange land held by an Adivasi holder.

(c) No sale or transfer in favour of a non-Adivasi can be sanctioned unless any Adivasi, residing within a radius of 5 kms is unwilling to buy it.

(d) If any transfer takes place in contravention of these provisions, the transfer will be declared invalid and the land will vest in Government. The land is to be restored to the original transferor, on condition that he shall pay back the original price received.

However, the Act suffered from two drawbacks:

(a) It provided for the restoration of lands transferred in contravention of legal provisions only.

(b) While it prohibited future transfers, it did not refer to the transfers that had already taken place.

Thus, the government passed another Act viz. the Maharashtra Restoration of Land to Scheduled Tribes Act (No. 14 of 75), which came into force from 1 November 1975. It provides for the restoration of lands transferred to non-tribal from 1 April 1957 to 6 July 1974, by way of sale, gift, exchange etc.[62]

Both Acts provided for the cases to be inquired into either on application by the tribal or suo-moto by the Collector. For the latter, the record of Rights of each plot of land was to be perused and any discrepancy therein was to be inquired into.

But even before they could go into operation, the Acts met with stiff resistance and stay orders on proceedings under the Acts were obtained from the Supreme Court. However in Lingappa Pocahanna versus State of Maharashtra and another; and in Kalu Gopya Banjari versus State of Maharashtra and another; the Supreme Court Bench of O. Chinappa Reddy, A.P. Sen and E.S. Venkatramiah on 4 December 1984, upheld the validity of Act 14/75. The judgement dismissed the appeals on various legal grounds and made some telling points noting 'that in the Constitution, the Scheduled Tribes, as a class require special protection against exploitation', It went on to say that, 'in the past 40 years, most of the tribal societies have come under attack by economically more advanced and politically more powerful ethnic groups...... the greedy land grabber and exploiter .... who infiltrated into tribal regions'. This 'triggered a struggle for land in which the aboriginal tribesmen were usually losers, and deprived of their ancestral lands, turned into impoverished landless labourers'. The judgement further stated that the concept of distributive justice is the 'removal of economic inequalities and the rectifying of the injustice resulting from dealings or transactions between unequals in society........ It means that those who have been deprived of their properties by unconscionable bargaining would be restored their property....... The impugned act is intended and meant as an instrument for alleviating oppression, redressing

62. Kulkarni Sharad : Alienation and Restoration of Adivasis' lands in Maharashtra, National Centre for Advocacy Studies publication.

bargaining imbalance, cancelling unfair advantage and generally overseeing and ensuring probity and fair dealing.'[63]

But, the actual implementation of these Acts shows how the very same powerful sections of society managed to ensure that the unfair advantage continued.

From the above, the most striking fact that emerges is that an overwhelming majority of the cases have been decided against the Adivasis. It is most revealing that out of a total of 45,534 cases that were filed under both Acts, land was restored in only 20,031 cases i.e. a success rate of only 43%. The reasons why cases were decided against the Adivasis or were dropped are listed below.

(i) The inquiries were conducted very callously. In many cases, the ALT did not refer to Section 32G proceedings at all to establish ownership and did not question the validity of the earlier proceedings. 'The Assistant Tahsildar has conducted the enquiry in the most callous manner. No permission under relevant provision of law was obtained before the transfer. The ALT had passed the order without making any inquiry and without recording the statements of the parties concerned.[65]

(ii) Ex-parte orders were passed. Adivasi applicants came regularly for court dates, but if he happened to miss a single date, orders were passed ex-parte. Further, even when the tribal went in appeal, the ex-parte orders were upheld as it was observed that, 'the tribal had no proof that the order was not served on him'.[66]

(iii) The ALT did not serve notices to all interested persons

63. Prabhu, Pradip., op cit.
65. Court Records. Maharashtra Revenue Tribunal, Mumbai, Case No 102/80, Heard and disposed of.
66. Court Records. Maharashtra Revenue Tribunal, Mumbai, Case No 56/77, Heard and disposed of.

TABLE 5 : District-wise valid transfers of land restored to ST Cultivators (as on 31.3.1999)[64]

District	*Act*	*Total No of cases*			*Area to be restored*			*Area actually restored*		
		Regd.	*Decided*	*Pending*	*Cases*	*STs.*	*Area-Ha*	*Cases*	*STs.*	*Area-Ha*
Thane	14/75	3,002	2,982	20	701	850	1,729	677	821	1,643
	35/74	2,799	2,798	1	962	1,039	1,350	955	1,021	1,342
Raigad	14/75	1,061	1,061	-	698	726	840	696	725	839
	35/74	1,008	1,008	-	719	729	703	718	728	702
Pune	14/75	65	65	-	47	47	66	47	47	66
	35/74	218	218	-	133	133	182	133	133	182
Nashik	14/75	1,665	1,664	1	869	870	1,339	862	865	1,321
	35/74	2,383	2,383	-	786	1,001	1,402	776	962	1,383
Jalgaon	14/75	1,163	1,163	-	747	1,132	1,755	646	1,031	1,385
	35/74	465	465	-	317	382	672	316	381	671
Dhule	14/75	4,771	4,771	-	1,205	1,566	4,083	1,102	1,437	3,883
	35/74	2,694	2,694	-	1,226	1,952	3,770	1,185	1,903	3,615
Ahmednagar	14/75	332	330	2	194	235	314	184	223	285
	35/74	576	575	1	340	426	483	327	413	458
Nanded	14/75	901	901	-	377	377	1,455	336	336	1,260
	35/74	1,086	1,086	-	186	188	528	176	169	488
Chandrapur	14/75	5,050	5,022	28	2,221	2,318	3,696	2,161	2,161	3,561
	35/74	77	77	-	14	14	17	14	14	17
Gadchiroli	14/75	1,649	1,646	3	1,082	1,140	1,453	1,063	1,063	1,366

64. Government of Maharashtra, Department of Revenue and Forests.

	35/74	1,169	1,167	2	348	360	613	342	348	535
Amravati	14/75	502	492	10	224	267	551	198	238	467
	35/74	788	785	3	522	534	1,786	521	531	1,782
Yavatmal	14/75	2,754	2,754	-	1,981	2,250	6,400	1,904	2,160	6,096
	35/74	75	75	-	52	56	121	49	52	115
Aurangabad	14/75	111	111	-	48	60	141	39	47	121
	35/74	31	30	1	8	12	24	6	8	21
Parbhani	14/75	352	350	2	211	274	614	165	181	422
	35/74	62	62	-	44	50	129	30	33	102
Jalna	14/75	-	-	-	-	-	-	-	-	-
	35/74	22	22	-	13	13	24	6	6	11
Nagpur	14/75	1,104	1,096	8	623	623	1,255	623	623	1,255
	35/74	304	304	-	180	180	360	180	180	360
Wardha	14/75	774	770	4	267	267	658	264	264	637
	35/74	-	-	-	-	-	-	-	-	-
Bhandara	14/75	4,997	4,993	4	2,818	2,893	2,500	2,627	2,746	2,266
	35/74	309	309	-	208	230	172	198	214	158
Akola	14/75	1,098	1,094	4	440	440	1,327	427	427	1,252
	35/74	73	73	-	33	33	75	32	32	73
Buldhana	14/75	72	69	3	29	51	80	23	40	66
	35/74	72	69	3	33	41	80	26	35	59
Total	14/75	31,423	31,334	89	14,782	16,386	30,256	14,044	15,435	28,191
	35/74	14,211	14,200	11	6,124	7,373	12,491	5,987	7,163	12,074
		45,634	**45,534**	**100**	**20,906**	**23,759**	**42,747**	**20,031**	**22,598**	**40,265**

to show cause. The Tahsildar had dropped the cases as 'the tribal was not available for statement'.[67]

(iv) The dates of decisions are/were not communicated to the tribals while the decision was intimated in advance to the non-tribal.

(v) Non-tribals eg. Hari Gulabdas Wani, managed to produce certificates that they were tribals - Mahadev Koli - and thus argued (successfully) that they were not to be considered as non-tribal transferees.[68]

(vi) Prior to Restoration proceedings, the non-tribals got the post tillers' day purchase declared ineffective; received back the land and sold it to the government. under the Ceiling Act, for which they received substantial compensation.[69] In such cases, the Restoration Acts were not applicable.

(vii) A non-tribal had a Bhil (tribal) mistress on whose name he transferred the land that he had appropriated from the tribal. He therefore argued successfully that the transfer was from a tribal to a tribal and not to a non-tribal.

(viii) Land consolidation measures which were poorly done, resulted in major alienations. We quote from the ruling of Tahsildar Palghar, in Pandu Dumada Paradhi versus Tukaram Balu Naik on 12.12.85 that, 'the Consolidation Officer has entered the name of the non-tribal without considering the position of the village records and the fact of possession'.

---

67. Court Records. Maharashtra Revenue Tribunal, Mumbai, Case No 235/77, Heard and disposed of.
68. Court Records. Maharashtra Revenue Tribunal, Mumbai, Case No 121/77, Heard and disposed of Court Records. Maharashtra Revenue Tribunal, Mumbai, Case No 121/77, Heard and disposed of.
69. Court Records. Maharashtra Revenue Tribunal, Mumbai, Case No 157/77, Heard and disposed of.

(ix) Tribals who have lost land to a trust cannot apply under the Restoration Act as a trust is not a non-tribal.

(x) Where tribal land has been taken over for non-agricultural purpose the Restoration Acts have been ineffective if:
   (a) The non-tribal transferee has transferred the land to another non-tribal before 15 March 71.
   (b) The transferred land has been put to non-agricultural use on or before 6 July 1974.

(xi) The Adivasis did not know of the Acts. There was little propaganda or information dissemination regarding the Act to the tribals themselves. Most cases were taken up suo-moto, and when the ALT called the Adivasi, he did not know why he was being called.

(xii) The non-tribals engaged lawyers in contravention of the Acts, who appeared for them and their *vakalatnamas* were subsequently removed from the case papers to make it appear as though no lawyer had appeared.

(xiii) Cases have been filled under wrong acts i.e. some cases that should have been registered under 14/75 have been registered under 35/74 and vice versa.[70]

The above makes it amply clear that the Restoration proceedings conducted by the ALT were totally to the detriment of the tribal. It was absolutely necessary that the ALT review the earlier Section 32G proceedings, which dealt with the purchase of land under the Tenancy Act. In fact this was the logic of the Restoration Acts, i.e. to redress the wrongs committed during the Land Reforms proceedings. Thus the nexus between the landed interests and the revenue

70. Prabhu, Pradip, 2002. *Land Alienation, Land Reforms and Tribals in Maharashtra* in *Land Reforms in India: Performance and Challenges in Gujarat and Maharashtra,* Ghanshyam Shah and Sah D.C.(ed.), Sage Publications.

authorities managed by and large to see that the purpose for which the Restoration Acts were promulgated was defeated.

The implications of a dropped case are of serious concern. In law, a dropped case implies that it has been legally examined and has no merit. It is important at this stage to recognize that an opportunity was created through the Restoration law for the tribal who was legally wronged in the implementation of the Tenancy, Ceiling and Prohibitory laws. A suo moto case was filed after prima facie legal grounds were made out in the records. The tribal was not even aware of the proceedings being initiated or being dropped. Hence, the act of closing a case is a judicial act and will operate as *res judicata,* meaning 'already adjudged' thereby effectively foreclosing any effort to re-examine the matter. In so doing, the tribal tenants have been doubly wronged through the fraudulent implementation of the Restoration Acts. The needle of responsibility necessarily points to the revenue officials and functionaries.[71]

What is also interesting is that in the relatively few cases where the lands were restored by the ALT to the tribals, the non-tribals appealed to the MRT. In the proceedings therein, the higher authorities managed to find minor discrepancies in the judgement at the lower lèvel, usually procedural in nature. Instead of using their discretion, the MRT capitalised on these minor discrepancies and passed judgements against the Adivasis. The grounds on which they did so are as below:

(a) The ALT had not enquired into the 'respondent's caste' i.e. that he is a tribal (177/79, MRT).

(b) The ALT had not taken the tribal's undertaking that he will cultivate the restored land personally and so Section 3(3) of the Act was contravened.

Thus in most cases, the revenue authorities were incapable of restoring the land to the Adivasis. The Restoration Acts

71. Prabhu, Pradip. Impact of Land Reforms in Maharashtra, op. cit.

have remained by and large ineffective. It is interesting to note that many more cases were filed under Act 14/75 except for three districts—Thane, Raigad and Nashik. This may indicate that either alienation of tribal land has decreased post-1975, or that such alienations are not being reported. But alienations continue to take place, and are occurring more rapidly under different guises (especially 99 year leases) where the records continue to show the Adivasi to be owner but possession is with the non-Adivasi. In such cases, the provisions of the Restoration Act are not applicable and therefore do not get reflected in the statistics. The fact that mass organizations and left parties are active in the three districts of Thane, Raigad and Nashik probably explains why cases continued to be filed under Act 35/74, after the campaign for initiating suo-moto proceedings ended.

It would be worth remembering that the Registers of Restoration Proceedings are not exhaustive of all alienations, post-1957. Since the Restoration proceedings were supposedly taken up after enquiring into discrepancies in the village level land records, (7/12 extracts), a similar counter-check was done for one village, chosen at random, viz. Aswali in Dahanu taluka of Thane district. This check revealed the presence of 32 irregularities. Of these, 21 came under the purview of the Restoration Acts. However, only 10 cases have been registered under the two acts. It thus appears likely that the nexus between landed interests and local administration was strong enough to conveniently leave out most cases.[72]

While Act 35/74 has no limitation period, the limitation period under Act 14/75 for applying for restoration is thirty years from the commencement of the Act. The Act came into force on 1 November 1975. Initially the prescribed limitation period was three years, but it was subsequently amended to thirty years. Thus as of today, the tribal who has lost his land

72. Prabhu, Pradip, 2002., op. cit..

prior to 1974, cannot avail of the provisions of this Act, as the limitation period ended on 30 October 2005. In many parts of tribal Maharashtra, tribal lands which had been alienated prior to 1974 are still in the possession of non-tribals. It is only in small pockets where social activists have been vigilant that the Restoration Act has been implemented. The Act therefore needs to be extended such that Adivasis in these areas can avail of the provisions of the Act.

Restoration of Lands in Jiwati Taluka—A Case Study

Jiwati taluka lies in Chandrapur district in the Vidarbha area of the state. The Adivasis belong to the Kolam and Gond tribes. During the 1973-74 drought, Banjara families (especially Mane) migrated from Naded, Parbhani and Latur. As the migrant non-tribal community was aggressive in nature, it found it easy to grab the lands of the meek Kolams.[73] Fifteeen thousand out of 20,000 Kolam families from about 100 villages of Jivati taluka of Chandrapur District lost their lands. Some Kolams left their lands and moved up into the hills, others into Andhra Pradesh, and some were even killed. Thirteen villages were totally abandoned. The process of illegal take-over is continuing even today. Till today the 7/12 extracts show Adivasis to be owners of the lands, but most of them are not in their possession.[74]

As per government records, the first complaint of land grabbing was filed in March 2003 before the Sub Divisional Officer (SDO), Rajura. An inquiry was initiated and 13 tribal families of Dharmaram, who had fled to Andhra Pradesh were identified as victims of land grabbing. An order was passed on 23 May 2003 to restore their lands. They were invited to take back their lands, but fearing for their lives,

---

73. Ghate, Rucha, Deepshila Mehra and Mukund Kulkarni. *A Study of Tribal Land Alienation and Restoration in Jiwati Taluka, Chandrapur District, Maharashtra State, India*, Shodh , May, 2006.
74. Interview with Vijay Siddheshwar, Mul, Chandrapur, May 2007.

only one person came forward to take actual possession. He too could not obtain his piece of land as he himself was unable to locate it after so many years. Since land survey records were not available, even with the government, his land could not be located. Meanwhile in Yellapur, a tribal woman was beaten up by non-tribals when she attempted to till her land. Thereafter, *Shramik Elgar*, an NGO, sent applications to the Tahsildar, and took out a *morcha* in June 2004, demanding that the 13 families from Dharmaram be returned their land. Shramik Elgar continued to pressurize the administration. Eventually the Collector was forced to issue written orders inviting complaints of land grabbing in 83 villages. Initially 99 applications were received, but in all *Shramik Elgar* filed 550 applications of 350 Kolam tribals and 200 Gond tribals.

The non-tribals hit back. Five armed attacks took place on the activists of *Shramik Elgar*. *Elgar* filed about 40-50 cases under Section 3(1)(v) of the Scheduled Tribes and Scheduled Castes Prevention of Atrocities Act. The Shiv Sena (Nandu Satam group) championed the side of the non-tribals. But *Shramik Elgar* continued its fight. It approached the High Court in a Writ Petition. The Court ordered the district authorities to take serious steps for conducting land surveys and to restore the land ownership to tribals. The alienated land in Dharmaram was handed over officially in December 2004. And by 21 May 2005, 190 families were physically restored their lands. The process of restoration continues till today and the majority of 550 applications that have been filed have been 'allowed'.

In Nandapa 27 families have been handed over possession of about 100 acres of land. They continue to cultivate these lands till date. Similarly, in Gadpandharwani, 16 families are in possession of the restored lands. But in Dharmaram, the 13 families who were handed over possession have actually lost their lands again to the same non-tribals from neighbouring Pittiguda village. The tribals are back to daily wage labour on their own lands at the rate of Rs.30 per day. Only one person has managed to retain half of his land. In Ambezari, six families were handed back land, but non-tribals grabbed it again. However, here *Shramik Elgar* with the help of the police managed to restore it once again. In Pallezari, a peculiar situation arose. Orders for restoration were passed in 14 cases. But due to ambiguity about the status of the lands (whether it falls within revenue or forest jurisdiction), the orders for restoration in eight cases have been withdrawn. Interestingly, after the orders were withdrawn, the non-tribals once again grabbed the lands and are now cultivating it.[75]

A Court order of March 2005 gave instructions to the authorities to provide agricultural implements, seeds, and other necessary items before the commencement of the sowing season. The Collector allocated a budget of Rs.14.57 lakhs for this. While houses and agricultural implements have been provided in some places, there are numerous complaints regarding poor construction or non-receipt of bullocks and ploughs.[76]

In nearby Zari taluka of Yavatmal, non-tribals belonging to the powerful Banjara community have also taken over tribal lands.[77]

4.3 Extent and Patterns of Tribal Land Alienation

The severity of land alienation is not uniform across the tribal areas. It varies from district to district and within a district itself. The variation across the state is shown in the following table:

75. Ghate Rucha et al., op. cit.
76. ibid.
77. Interview with Vijay Siddheshwar, Mul, Chandrapur, May 2007.

TABLE 5[78] : Severity of tribal land alienation

Name of district	*Talukas where land alienation is severe*	*Talukas where land alienation is negligible*
Thane	Dahanu, Wada, Palghar, Shahapur	Jawhar, Mokhada, Talasari
Nashik	Dindori, Igatpuri, Nashik, Baglan	Peth, Surgana, Kalwan
Dhule	Nandurbar, Shirpur, Sakri, Taloda, Shahada	Akrani, Addalkuwa, Nawapur
Ahmednagar	Akola	
Yavatmal	Kelapur, Yavatmal	
Nanded	Kinwat	
Chandrapur	Warora, Rajura	
Amravati		Chikhaldara, Dharni
Gadchiroli		Sironcha, Aheri, Etapalli, Dhanora, Kurkheda, Armori, Charmoshi

A recent study shows that while the majority of land alienation involves the loss of as little as one acre, in some cases more than 5 acres too have been alienated. It is interesting to note that in 84% of these cases, the tribal has lost the entire area of land.

TABLE 6[79] : Extent of Area alienated

Extent of Area alienated	*%age of cases*
1 to 2 acres	43%
3 to 5 acres	33%
Over 5 acres	24 %

The major forms of alienation were sale (51.49%) and lease (31.36%). The monetary recompense that may have been

78. Tribal Research and Training Institute, Pune : A Study to determine the Extent of Tribal Land Alienation in Maharashtra State, 1987-88.
79. Prabhu, Pradip, 2007b, op. cit.

received was mainly to meet consumption needs (40.8%) and for debt redemption (25.89%).[80]

It is interesting to examine who the current title holders of the alienated lands are. The following table seeks to provide an answer:

TABLE 7[81] : Current Title Holders of Alienated Tribal Lands

Current Title Holders of Tribal Lands	*Shahapur*	*Dahanu*	*Total*
Original Landlords/Heirs	24	10	34
New Purchasers from Landlords	11	30	41
Others	13	0	13
Original Tribal Tenant Cultivator	2	10	12

The above table indicates that title to land particularly that of land cultivated by unrecorded tenant cultivators, is rapidly passing on to new buyers. The hitherto value of the land, though suppressed before sale, has become real for new purchasers who have spent hard cash to procure the land. They are unaware of the history of the area and therefore take steps to get possession even with the attendant conflict as long as it is manageable.[82]

4.4 Additional tenancy related issues

Un-recorded Tenancies pre 1957 which continue to date

The tenants also had in their possession patches of high-land on which they cultivated pulses and oil-seeds for home consumption and grazed their cattle. However these lands, which were fairly extensive, were never recorded in the names of the tenants, and it was presumed that for every acre of rent yielding land, the tenant could occupy and take produce from a proportionate amount of grass-land. As tenancy on these lands was never recorded, they remained

80. Government of Maharashtra, Tribal Research and Training Institute, Pune, 1987-88., op. cit..
81. Prabhu, Pradip, 2007b, op. cit.
82. Prabhu, Pradip, 2007b, op. cit.

in the names of the landlords as *'varkas'* or grass-lands. The landlords ensured that these lands never came under the purview of any tenancy legislation.

This situation prevails in almost every village in the tribal areas. Considerable tracts of land have been in the possession of tenants for one or two generation, but their names have never been entered in the land records. Though the law requires that the Talathi verify the 'correctness' of the entries in the 7/12 extracts and the de-facto situation of possession every year, such verification is either not done or perfunctorily made. The landlord's name is on the records, even while the tenant retains possession and use of the land. As these lands in interior villages become more accessible and marketable with the building of roads, landlords sell these lands to third parties on the basis of the position in the records. The non-recorded tenants are then evicted by the new owners and the tenants have a very weak legal case to recover these lands as their names are not in the records as tenants in possession of land. This is a serious situation that needs immediate attention. Such situations exist in almost every tribal village of Thane district and particularly severe in the villages of Ambesari, Chalni, Nimbapur, Bandghar, Raipur, Ashta, Bendgaon, Saiwan, Dharampur, Vanai (Dahanu taluka); Ozar, Morchechapada (Jawhar taluka). In Raipur village (Dahanu taluka) 22 tribal cultivators are cultivating about 58 hectares of land. In addition, there are about 16–20 ha of grassland from which the tribals are taking produce for generations. This phenomenon is widespread and is spread across the village in different hamlets.

The stories of two villages in Thane and Raigad districts where Adivasi unrecorded tenants have struggled for their lands are given below:

Vanai Gadagpada – unrecorded no more

Vanai Gadagpada is a hamlet situated in Dahanu Taluka of Thane district. It is inhabited by approximately 25 families of Warlis. Many of these Adivasis were the former tenants of the erstwhile landlord, Shri Darji. Some of these lands were sold to some of the tenants under the Tenancy Act, but a large area (approximately 20 acres) of land continued to be in the possession of 20 non-recorded tenants. The land records did not show their cultivation; neither did the tribals have any proof of tenancy. These tenants had also constructed their houses in a cluster covering an area of approximately 4 acres. As the original tenant was one Gadag, the hamlet was called Gadagpada.

The original landlord, Shri Darji had meanwhile, about 60 years ago, mortgaged the land. The possession of the tenants however remained undisturbed. In 1980, Shri Darji received back the title over the lands from the mortgagee by virtue of a Court decree. Even so Shri Darji never visited the lands. Meanwhile the land became attractive as the irrigation canal of the Surya Project had been constructed alongside the lands. In 1994 Shri Darji tried to evict the tribal families. On 29.3.94, he along with some others, armed with sickles attacked the hamlet. They broke the cactus compound and uprooted the wooden pillars of a '*mandav*' (or pandal) . They cut the rope supporting the cradle of a sleeping child who fell to the floor. They even tried to burn the houses of the tribals. However they were unsuccessful as the villagers chased them out of the village.

In December 1994, Shri Darji again tried to enter some of the lands that were lying vacant (approx. 8 acres) and construct a shed thereupon. However, the villagers who by then were organized under the banner of the *Kashtakari Sanghatna,* successfully prevented him from doing so. Nor was he able to enter the lands to survey them. He then filed a civil suit seeking an injunction against the villagers. However, the Court ruled that possession lay with the tribals and therefore did not grant the injunction. He thereupon appealed in the Sessions Court, who in 1998 upheld the order of the lower Court. The matter continued in the lower court on the issue of title. Meanwhile the tribals continued in possession of all the lands, including that which was left vacant.

Realising that he had lost on both counts—i.e. in the Courts and on the ground—Shri Darji approached the villagers for a settlement. As the tribals, had no documentary evidence to establish ownership rights in a Court of law, they agreed to come to a settlement. By virtue of the settlement made on 8 May 1998,

1. Shri Darji was permitted to survey the lands, and draw a map, indicating the ground reality.
2. Shri Darji agreed to give to the tribals the lands in their possession, both under cultivation and the area of the village which included their house sites and (*vadas*) (or kitchen gardens) around the houses and a portion of the lands on the hillside adjacent to the canal for their sanitary use.
3. The tribals would not be granted the lands free of cost, but would purchase the same under the provisions of the Tenancy Act.
4. The tribals agreed to permit Shri Darji to take possession of the remaining vacant lands.
5. Shri Darji agreed that while taking possession of these vacant lands, and constructing a fence around the same, the access roads traditionally used by the tribals would be left undisturbed, including a road towards the hillside to allow them access the hillside for their sanitary needs.

Since coming to this agreement, Shri Darji has taken possession of approximately eight acres of vacant land. About 20 acres continues to be in the possession of the Adivasis. A pursis was filed in the Court in the light of the settlement. However, the matter is still pending due to a delay in the survey work. Consequently, the process of transferring the title on to the name of the tribals remains to be completed.

Kelad Thakurwadi – Taming the Khot

Similarly, in Kelad Thakurwadi, Roha Taluka, Raigad district, the Thakur tribals were tenants of a powerful landlord (*Khot*) for generations. They used to pay rent of 12 quintals of paddy per year. While six of them were recorded as tenants, the others were not. The Khot tried to evict them from the lands and had initiated legal proceedings against them. The Khot had got the tribals to sign false documents stating that they were relinquishing all rights to the land. The landlord had also obtained a Court order in his favour.

In the late 1990s, the *Sarvahara Jan Andolan* then took up a systematic campaign to protect the rights of these non-recorded tenants. On the ground itself it physically prevented any attempt to evict the tenants. Demonstrations were held in the Taluka and district place. A case was filed against the landlord under the Atrocities Act. The Khot's other malpractices in the timber trade were also exposed. The issue was raised in the State Assembly. Influential political leaders mediated and applied pressure on the landlord. After a prolonged struggle, the Khot parted with 55 acres of his land.[83]

Sale of Tenancy Lands in the Name of the Eldest Son

During Section 32 G proceedings, for the sake of convenience, the sale of tenancy lands has been done in the name of the eldest son or the literate son, while the other brothers retained possession and use of the lands. They even contributed their share of the sale price. But in many cases, only the name of the eldest son was entered in the Section 32 M certificate. Consequently only his name has entered as owner of the jointly cultivated lands. As there was no ill-will between the joint holders, no-one bothered about the administrative lapse. However, on the death of the person mentioned in the records as 'owner', the names of only his heirs enter the records as owners and the other co-parceners are excluded from any rightful title to the lands. In recent years, this has led to internal conflicts within a village, where the subsequent heirs

83. Interview with Ulka Mahajan, Sept 2007.

have even filed suits for eviction of the other brothers or their children, or criminal cases of theft (eg. Kalamgaon in Mokhada taluka). As a result, the other rightful owners of the land are evicted. This is a serious problem in most tribal villages and needs to be addressed with alacrity.

Non-sale of Widow's, Minor's, Inami, Temple Lands in the Possession of Tenants

The BTAL Act did not permit the sale of land to the tenant where the landlord was a widow, minor, *inamdar*[84] or a *devasthan*[85] . However, even after the status of the landlord as widow or minor has changed, the sale to the tenant has not taken place (eg. Bandhan village of Vikramgad taluka). However, these lands are sometimes subsequently sold to third parties on the basis of the position in the records. The tenants then face eviction by the new owners. In Morchyachapada, (taluka Jawhar), 57.14.17 ha of land belonging to the erstwhile landlords Ramesh Purshottam Ponda have not been transferred to the tenants belonging to 60-70 Adivasi nuclear families. In Bendgaon and Dehne villages (Dahanu taluka) lands were not transferred on to the Adivasi's name despite the payment of purchase price ten years previous. The fact that *Devasthan inami*[86] has still not been abolished has implied that the Adivasis from Adoshi, Shirasgaon, Dolhara and Khodala of Mokhada taluka have failed to get their lands transferred on to their names.

Deliberate Deletion of Tribal's Name during Land Consolidation Proceedings

There are innumerable cases where the Adivasis's name has been deleted during Land Consolidation proceedings. Prior to the scheme, the tribal may have been in possession of a

84. One who possess Land.
85. Temple.
86. Temple as the one who possess the land.

much larger area of land, which was considerably reduced in the Land Consolidation Scheme that was prepared. The beneficiary at the expense of the tribal is invariably a wealthy influential non-tribal. As the Scheme was prepared without the participation of the Village community, as required by law, the unsuspecting tribal continues to cultivate the land till the time he suddenly faces eviction by the landlord or a third party to whom the original landowner has sold the land.

In *Bendgaon* village, one Deu Balu Bongya has had his holdings reduced from 1.256 to 1.047 ha (a loss of 0.21 ha). In *Dhanoshi* village of Jawhar taluka, the share of the non-tribal cultivator (Smt. Tendulkar) increased from about 4 acres to about 20 acres after Consolidation, while that of the tribal (Jogari) reduced to only a few *gunthas*[87]. In village *Vanai* (Dahanu taluka), the names of the tribal cultivators (Ranju Chavan and others) totalling about 8.31 acres has been removed from the records of the lands that had been sold to them via the Tenancy Act. The landlord on to whose name the land has been transferred has now sold the land to a third party claiming clear title. When the Adivasi applied for rectification of the Consolidation proceedings, the TILR[88] has tried to sort out the matter by apportioning equal shares to the tribal and non-tribal, without actually apportioning to the tribal the total amount of land that was in his name prior to the Consolidation proceedings.

Distribution of Government Wastelands

There are large areas of government wastelands in every village of the State. Some of these lands were distributed to landless persons in the 1970s. Each person was granted one to two and a half acres of land.

A study of 24 villages in the state showed that 24.5% of beneficiaries were found to belong to Scheduled Tribes and

87. Guntha is a measure of area. 1 Gunta = 121 square yards = 101.17 square metres = 2.5 cents. 40 Gunthas make an acre,
88. Taluka Inspector of Land Record.

thus the distribution was in line with the priority norm accorded for the selection of beneficiaries from weaker sections. But sub-zonal figures indicate that the norm has been violated in the scarcity zone and in the west coastal plains, where 79.31% and 56.6% respectively of beneficiaries were non-SC and non-ST. However, across the state, STs received proportionately less area of land than other beneficiaries: 24.5% STs received only 19.74% of land distributed.[89]

Additionally large tracts of government land are in the possession of cultivators. Many of these are non-tribals, some even large landowners. Even so, a large number of Adivasis are cultivating such lands. In Thane district, the landless persons in the 'jungalpatti' have occupied forest land that is in close proximity to their villages. However, the landless and marginal farmers in the coastal strip have occupied government wastelands. Some of these are beneficiaries of the Land distribution Schemes, who have extended their cultivation on to the vacant non-distributed government wasteland. Some of these cultivations have been noted as 'encroachments on government land' in the I(E) Registers kept with the *Talathis*[90]. However, most of these are not. The Maharashtra Government passed a Resolution on 28 November1991 regularising agricultural encroachments on government wastelands that were in existence on 14 April 1990. This Government resolution was framed to address the burning problem of encroachments on *gairan*[91] lands by dalits in Marathwada. However, the encroachments by tribals on all government lands are also covered under the said government resolution. But till date not a single encroachment has been regularized.

89. Iyer, Gopal, Distribution of Government Wastelands in Western India, in *Land Reforms in India: Performance and Challenges in Gujarat and Maharashtra,* Shah Ghanshyam and Sah D.C.(ed); Sage Publications, 2002.
90. *Talathis* are the principal village officials.
91. Waste land.

4.6 Implementation of Ceiling Laws

The Maharashtra Agricultural Land (Ceiling on Holdings) Act 1961 imposing ceiling on holdings became operative on 26 January 1961. The ceilings prescribed in the act were revised in 1972 and the revised ceiling came into force from 2 October 1975. A study showed that 80.5% of the landowners from whom land was acquired belonged to the upper and middle castes. However, land from large landowners among the lower castes and tribals (4.1%) were also acquired.[92] In Ijardari in the erstwhile Nizam area of Chandrapur, 1,200 acres of land were acquired from one tribal landlord, Raju Atram.

Under the ceiling act, according to state statistics, 0.93 lakh tribals were granted 1.24 lakh ha of ceiling surplus land.[93] A major portion (about 64%) of this distribution took place in the Konkan and Amravati revenue divisions. In Morbe village of Raigad district, the erstwhile landless Scheduled Tribe allottees were now landowners. While earlier they were indebted to local moneylenders they were now free from their clutches. They had become members of the Primary Agricultural Co-operative Society from where they got inputs in the form of seeds and fertilizers though some of them continued to engage in part-time wage labour.[94] In Adharne village (Sateri, Batemal and Hedoshi Thakurwadi) of Pen taluka, Raigad district, 63 Adivasis were beneficiaries of 363 acres under the distribution of Ceiling lands. However, in reality no land was handed over to them. The *Shramik Kranti Sanghatna* organized the Adivasis and forced the administration to put them in possession of the said lands. Maps of the lands were drawn for the first time and the Adivasis were given actual possession of the lands. Similarly

92. ibid.
93. Prabhu, Pradip: Impact of Land Reforms in Maharashtra, op. cit.
94. Iyer, Gopal K., op. cit..

Adivasis from Cherfalwadi and Paned Katkarwadi also received similar lands.[95]

However, the general situation with respect to distribution of surplus land is dismal:

(a) In many areas, the distribution of ceiling surplus land has been only on paper. Tribals are in possession of land documents which indicate that they are owners of surplus lands, but the lands have never been handed over to them. In Murbad taluka of Thane district, Katkaris who are beneficiaries of this scheme have made applications to the TILR for survey and possession of the lands. However, the lands declared surplus bear the same survey number as the original land and is shown in the records to be a part (*paiki*) of the same survey number. No gat book maps (gat is the new name for land survey numbers. So a gat book map refers to a map of the particular parcel of land) are available for a part (*paiki*) of a survey number. As no demarcation has taken place by the revenue authorities, the survey department is not in a position to measure out that specific part which has been allotted to the beneficiary.[96] Similar applications are lying pending in many survey offices, including that of 25 Adivasis of Karanjvira village of Dahanu taluka.

(b) The lands declared surplus under the ceiling act are in the possession of unrecorded tenants. If the land is to be handed over to the beneficiary, it will involve the dispossession of another tribal and subsequent conflict in the village. Thus such land distribution remains on paper. However, it is expected that in the coming years, the anomaly will result in internal conflicts between tribals in the village.

(c) Landless tribals in one village are given ceiling land

95. Interview with Surekha Dalvi, Mumbai, January 2008.
96. Interview with Indavi Tulpule, Murbad, December 2007.

grants in a distant village; thereby the land effectively remains in the hands of the landlord.

(d) The land obtained under the ceiling is waste land unfit for cultivation. Once the area to be declared surplus was decided by the authorities, it was the landlord's prerogative to decide on which land to be handed over.

(e) Paradoxically, some persons who have received possession of fairly good land under the Ceiling Act are not cultivating it. As they were not traditionally agriculturists they have not shown much interest in cultivating it. This is especially so with the Adivasis of Chandrapur district.[97]

The conclusion is that distribution of ceiling lands is one of the weakest aspects of the implementation of the land ceiling programme. It has had very marginal impact on the economic condition of the beneficiaries. This is borne out by villages studied by the IAS probationers of the Lal Bahadhur Shastri National Academy of Administration in 1994.

4.7 Sops to the Adivasis

In 2004, the Government of Maharashtra began a new scheme 'to provide a permanent means of production to the Adivasis'. The *Bhoomiheen Daridraya Reshekal Adivasinche Sabalikaran va Svabhiman Yojana* envisages the purchase of land by the Tribal Welfare Department in the open market and the distribution of the same to landless Adivasis on a grant-cum-loan basis. It is expected that Rs.10 crores will be allocated annually for the implementation of the scheme. A beneficiary must be below the poverty line and will be eligible to a maximum of 4 acres dry land or 2 acres irrigated land. The beneficiary will receive a grant amounting to 50% of the purchase price of the land. The remaining 50% will be in the form of a loan

97. Interview with Vijay Siddheshwar, Mul, Chandrapur, May 2007.

to be repaid in installments in ten years, first installment beginning after two years of sanction of the loan. Priority is to be accorded to Primitive Tribal Groups, Deserted Women and Widows. The Scheme is to be implemented in 15 districts. Six districts were identified in 2003-04 (Thane, Gadchiroli, Yavatmal, Nashik , Nandurbar and Amravati). As only Rs.1 crore was sanctioned in 2003-04, each district received Rs.16.66 lakhs. This includes both the grant and loan components.

If the cost of land is taken to be a conservative Rs.. 50,000 per acre, then Rs. 2 lakhs will be required for one beneficiary. Thus a maximum of 8 persons in the entire district will benefit from this scheme in one year. Therefore the inability of this scheme to address the problem of landlessness is quite apparent.

4.8 Tenancy Reforms – A Conclusion

Eminent writers have concluded that the implementation of tenancy legislation has been tardy.[98] As the landlords threw the Adivasi tenants out of their lands, the implementation of tenancy legislation had the opposite effect to what was intended. Further, the extent of simultaneous land alienation was so high that it negated the effect of the land grants under the provisions of the law.

The Restoration Acts which were enacted to undo exactly these anomalies were systematically made ineffective. The failure in the implementation of the restoration of tribal lands can be attributed to the Revenue department. The executive arm of the government, mainly the lower functionaries, can and has consciously and willfully defeated the will of the legislature and the functionaries have gone unscathed. In every case of progressive land legislation, their complicity is evident, as they spare no efforts to circumvent the laws through acts of commission or omission. Land being such a

98. Iyer, Gopal K, 2002, op cit.

complex issue, few people other than the revenue officers themselves understand the finer points of law. The continued capitalist intrusion into the Adivasi areas in the form of capitalist agriculture and 'development' on the one hand, and the exploitation of the recreation 'needs' of the capitalist and its attendant classes on the other, has fuelled the ever increasing demand for cheap land. The revenue authorities have fallen prey to these 'money bags' who fall at their feet to guide them how to circumvent the law. Ways and means are devised such that either the law is circumvented or that an impression is created that the law is being followed. It is in this intransigence of the state's functionaries and the perceived inability of the state to ensure that the law is implemented by its minions, that the roots of alienation of Adivasi people can be located. Additionally, the legislature has been slow to rectify anomalies in enactments, and has introduced new amendments and Rules which are regressive in nature. The Adivasis are compromised further as the legislators introduce loopholes in the law under the pressure of the landed elites. Land reform laws become like other pro poor statutes, devoid of teeth.

Consequently, post-independence land reform laws were sadly still-born for a good section of expectant Adivasis as their premises, interpretation and implementation remained imprisoned in the iron clad frame of the relationship between the landlord and the Adivasi cultivator that had evolved during the colonial period. The process of land reform followed the colonial matrix and hence the colonial praxis around land continued well into the early independence period to the immense detriment of the Adivasi cultivator. Instead of the tenant becoming the owner of the land on 'tillers day', it resulted in the alienation of a good proportion of the lands of the tribal tenants to land owning elite groups.[99]

99. Prabhu, Pradip, 2007a, op. cit.

4.9 Atrocities Act

The Scheduled Castes and Scheduled Tribes (Prevention of Atrocities) Act 1989, popularly called the Atrocities Act, has been used extensively in Maharashtra to seek justice. However sections 3(1)(iv) and 3(1)(v) which deal with the 'wrongful occupation or cultivation of any land owned or allotted' to an SC or ST and 'interference with the enjoyment of (his) rights over any land' have been used very sparingly. Of the total number of 1,093 cases that had been filed during 1991-94, only 4 had been registered under section 3(1)(iv) and 28 under section 3(1)(v). Of these, 12 are in Nagpur division, 10 in the Konkan and 5 each in Nashik and Amravati divisions.[100] The cases filed in Jiwati taluka of Chandrapur district, post-2004, are not included in these statistics.

Svashasan Act

To the best of our knowledge, this Act too has not been used anywhere in the State to prevent alienation of land or its restoration. In Bendgaon village of Dahanu taluka of Thane district, a resolution was passed in the Gram Sabha regarding restoration of alienated land in the year 2000. However, lacunae in the Maharashtra Svashasan Act (which was not in consonance with the Central Act) and lack of effective follow-up did not result in the actual restoration of the lands. However, subsequently in 2003, the Act has been amended making it 'incumbent on the Collector to initiate necessary appropriate action for prevention..... or restoration of the land' if the Gram Sabha has so recommended to the Collector.

As mentioned earlier, the Svashasan Act has been used to prevent the construction of the Mumbai-Talasari Express Highway. The proposed gas bottling plant at Velgaon in Palghar taluka of Thane district has also been stalled because the Gram Sabha has refused permission for the same. The matter is pending in the Mumbai High Court.

---

100. Government of Maharashtra, Tribal Research and Training Institute. *An Evaluation Study of the Atrocities on STs in Maharashtra*, 1995.

5

Forest Land

The entire process of settlement of forest rights took place largely on paper. No settlement took place when the former princely states merged with Independent India. Large scale alienation of land to non-tribals without effective redress and displacement without proper rehabilitation has also pushed the Adivasis into the forest where they have begun to cultivate degraded forest lands.

Over the years, the Forest Department has recognized that protection of the forests is not possible without the active support of the Adivasis. As far back as 1884, the Forest Department therefore decided to allot *Dali* plots to Adivasis in Raigad District. Similarly, as per a recommendation in 1895, Woodland Plots were allotted in Thane District, and Fire-line, Pillar-line and Agro-silvi plots were allotted in Nandurbar (formerly Dhule) district. The allottees were expected to protect the adjacent forests (especially from fires) while cultivating the land allotted to them. However, till date these lands have still not been transferred on to the names of the cultivating tribals.[101]

5.1 Woodland Plots and Eksali Plots

In 1938, in Thane District alone there were 11,374 woodland plots covering 28,972 acres. Immediately after World War II,

101. Campaign for Survival and Dignity, 2003. *Endangered Symbiosis: Evictions and India's Forest communities.*

as part of the 'Grow More Food' campaign, Adivasis were encouraged to cultivate forest lands. Most of the woodland plots were converted into *Eksali* Plots (i.e. one-year leases). In addition, other wastelands were also converted into *Eksali* Plots. On 22 March 1969, the State Government issued a resolution to regularize all *Eksali* Plots. However, since the resolution had not been implemented, one Vishwanath Jadhav approached the Bombay High Court, which specifically stated on 13 February 1987 that the Forest Department cannot take refuge under the Forest Conservation Act (since the decision to regularize was prior to 1980), and that therefore the 10,000 *Eksali* plots covering 32,000 acres in Sholapur taluka should be regularized. However, till date in Thane District alone, 16,960 *Eksali* plots are yet to be regularized. On 19 November 1998, the Mumbai High Court ordered the Maharashtra Government to complete the process of regularization of all plots in Thane district within one year. However, the government has not complied with the orders till date.[102]

Dali Plots

During Peshwa Rule, the system of *Dali* cultivation on hilly lands was prevalent and a tax was levied on it. *Dali,* which is a mode of preparing the *'warkas'* land (what is this?), by burning in-site vegetation and ploughing or hand digging and sowing in the burnt areas, is done mainly by forest based tribes like Thakars, Katkaris and Mahadev Koli, but also by Maratha and Mahar farmers.

This cultivation was formally stopped around 1878. A number of petitions were made by *dali* cultivators to the government. Thus in 1887, the Forest Settlement Officer of Kolaba had stated before the Bombay Forest Commission that, '..... the *Dali* is not only a possible means but almost the only possible means of improving the forests.....' and suggested that plots should be assigned to Thakars, Katkaris

---

102. ibid.

and Dhangars ...to... provide them with a suitable means of livelihood....'.. *Dali* lands were leased out to a community, though the actual lease title was made in name of the local headman or '*naik*'. The *dali* lease was renewed annually and regular passbooks were issued by the Forest Department, which recorded the names of fellow community men and had a map of the *dali* plot and a schedule of the land cultivated. A separate written agreement between the cultivators and the Forest Department was made and a license to cultivate was also issued.

On 14 January 1970, the Maharashtra Government passed a resolution to regularize all *dali* plots on the names of the beneficiaries. In Raigad district, there are a total of 458 plots with 4,872 plot holders covering 12,919.54 ha. Of these, the Forest department has deforested 11,389.51 ha (88.15%) but has till date transferred only 1,405.859 ha (10.88%) to the revenue department.

However, once again the resolution was not implemented. Despite the fact that the government resolution is prior to the 1980 Conservation Act, and that the Central Government has stated that no compensatory afforestation is necessary, the *dali* plots were not regularized. In fact, the Attorney General on 15 January 1999 clearly mentioned in the Supreme Court that such permission is not necessary. Meanwhile the Maharashtra Government sent proposals for regularization to the Central government which understates the area under cultivation for regularization. While the 1971 GR states that 5924 *dali* plot-holders with an area of 11,042 ha are eligible for regularization, the proposal of the Maharashtra government in 1999-2000 proposes only 4,804 plot-holders with only 4,359 hectares.[103]

Fireline, Pillar line and Agro Silvi plots

These are to be found in parts of Nandurbar district (Shahada taluka). As mentioned earlier, these were allotted to the tribals to assist in forest protection. Resolutions to regularize these

103. ibid

plots were made around 50 years ago; however, till date the resolutions have not been implemented.[104]

Forest Plots

Besides the above mentioned plots, the Adivasis continued to cultivate land in the forests. As the lands belonged to the Forest Department, these were treated as encroachments by the administration. Over the years, some of these lands were regularized as per government orders. However, there were also attempts made from time to time to evict the cultivators. But sustained resistance from the Adivasis and the likely political fallout of evictions forced the state to regularize these cultivations.

Maharashtra passed two Resolutions in 1978 and 1979, ordering the regularization of cultivation on fallow lands, forest lands and grazing lands by tribals and non-tribals below the poverty line. However, the Resolutions were never implemented, and the cultivators continued to face harassment and eviction by the forest department.

In 1982, Adivasis from Dhule district approached the Supreme Court seeking implementation of the said Resolutions. First in 1982, and later in 1986, tribals from Thane District also filed a Writ Petition in the Supreme Court (W.P. 1778/86: Pradip Prabhu vs. State of Maharashtra) with the same prayer. In 1995, the Supreme Court passed an order directing the State of Maharashtra to appoint responsible officers in different districts to examine the claims of Adivasis who are in possession of land and decide their claims for regularization in accordance with law and the instructions issued by the Government of India on 18 September 1990. Earlier in 1991, the Supreme Court in the said case had held that 'the competent authority may even in cases where the claim is not supported by documents make an appropriate inquiry, receive evidence and then come to accept the claim'. It is to be noted that the 1979 Maharashtra Government Resolution itself states that 'all other forms of evidence' are

104. ibid

admissible when deciding the eligibility of a claim. In the course of the Inquiry in WP 1778/86, procedures were also laid down regarding the conducting of inquiries, acceptance of oral evidence and affidavits in addition to documentary fine receipts, and the involvement of the village community and *panchas* in assessing the year of cultivation.

In 2002, following the infamous 3 May 2002 letter of the Inspector General of Forests, the Maharashtra government initially issued on 4 September 2002 a circular regarding the formation of a 'time-bound Action Plan to remove unauthorized encroachments from Forest lands'. Eviction notices were issued to thousands of cultivators. In Amravati district, elephants were used to trample on peoples' cultivation. However, subsequently due to sustained pressure from various quarters, the Maharashtra government was forced to reconsider its stand. On 17 September 2002, it issued a temporary stay on the eviction of encroachments by Adivasis.[105]

On 10 October 2002, in pursuance of the pattern adopted for regularization in Amravati district (where 872 Land Certificates were issued in 2001 by the Collector who had devised a community-based inquiry procedure into claims for regularization), village level and taluka level committees were appointed to decide on eligibility of encroachments made by Adivasis.

The State Government has reported that about 73,000 ha of land were under encroachments. However, the actual area is many times more. In Nandurbar district alone, 44,000 tribals have made claims for regularization, while in Thane and Nashik districts about 30,000 claims each have been made. In Chandrapur district, 650 claims were declared eligible. The process of inquiry as per the Government resolution of 10 October 2002 is still in progress, as no final decision has been taken by the District level committees. In some areas, the inquiry has taken place as per the norms prescribed in the G.R. i.e. in open Gram Sabhas, oral evidence

105. ibid.

including that of the Gram Sabha has been relied upon and eligibility criteria have been followed. However, in many areas, in contravention of the conditions laid down in the G.R., only documentary evidence of fine receipts has been accepted, and the inquiry has not taken place in the Gram Sabha. These claims were rejected. This is especially so in the Vidarbha region.

Taking the wind out of the Windmills – a struggle to prevent privatization of forest land

Adivasis of Sakri taluka of Dhule district have been in possession of and have been cultivating forest lands for a long time. Their cultivations are eligible to be regularized under the criteria laid down by the government. However, instead of determining these rights, the government diverted 212.56 ha of forest land for the use of Suzlon Energy Ltd. to set up windmills for the construction of a 225 MW Wind Power Project. Much of this land is under cultivation by Adivasis. The project involved the cutting down of thousands of trees. The local Adivasis under the leadership of the *Satyashodak Gramin Kashtakari Sabha* opposed the setting up of the windmills, tooth and nail. The workers from the company were physically prevented from stepping on to the land. Massive mobilizations took place in the Taluka and the district town. The *Jagatikikaran Virodhi Kruti Samiti* extended active support to the local struggle. Suzlon tried to pressurize the Adivasis by forcing the administration to initiate externment proceedings against its leader. But the Adivasis did not flinch. They continued their struggle. The externment proceedings appear to have been stalled. The Adivasis continue to cultivate their lands.[106]

5.2 Adivasis living in Forest Villages

There were 447 forest villages in the state, which were converted to revenue villages in 1977. However, 73 forest villages in Akrani Taluka of Nandurbar district have retained

106. Interview with Kishore Dhamale, Mumbai, January 2008.

TABLE 8 : Population and Land status of Tribal and Other Traditional Communities residing in National Parks and Wildlife Sanctuaries in Maharashtra

Sl No.	*National Parks (NP) / Wild Life Sanctuaries (WLS)*	*Tribal / Traditional Communities*	*Population within Park (1991 census)*	*Area under encroachment*	*Remarks*
	MTR WL Circle and 3 other sanctuaries				
1.	GuganMal NP	No habitation			
2.	Ambabarwa WLS	Info not available	1,408	0.52 sq. kms.	
3.	*Melghat WLS*	*Korku (80%) Gawli, Nihal, Balahi, Rathya, Halbi, Vanjari, Gond, Burad*	*7,155 (2002) - 22 villages*	*110 cases are pending*	*Korkus and Nihals depend on agriculture. These were formely forest villages, which became revenue villages in 1977. Three of the 22 villages already relocated. Rehabilitation of other villages planned.*
4.	Narnala WLS	No habitation			
5.	Wan WLS	Information not available	2,968 (7 villages)	0.49 sq. kms.	4 villages to be relocated.
6.	Karanja Sohal Black Buck WLS	Information not available			0.54 sq. kms of *malki* land in WL
7.	Lonar WLS	No habitation		31% of WL under agriculture	
8	Malvan Marine Sanctuary	Information not available			
			2,696		

	Nagpur WL Circle				
9.	*Nawegaon NP*	*Gond*	*494: 6 hamlets*	*1.8 q. kms.*	
10.	*Pench NP*	*Gond, Dhimar*	*400 in Phulzari (0.95 sq. km)*	*4.25 sq. kms.*	
11.	*Tadoba NP*	*No habitation within*			*2 villages relocated*
12.	*Andhari WLS*	*Gond, Madia, Gowari*	*3,195*		*6 villages. Large areas are revenue forest lands. Most inhabitants practice rain fed farming on marginal lands*
13.	Bor Game Sanctuary	Information not available	959 : 5 hamlets		10 sites relocated
14.	*Bhamragad WLS*	*Madia Gond*			*Shifting cultivation, kasari and hill millet.*
15.	*Chaprala WL San*	*Gond, Madia Gond, Kevat*	*3,263: 6 villages*		*Practise rain fed agriculture*
16.	*Nagzira WL Game Sanctuary*	*Gond*	*349: 2 villages*		*One village relocated*
17.	Tipeshwar WLS	Information not available	3 villages		Agricultural land of 3 other villages
	Nashik WL Circle				
18.	*Aner Dam WLS*	*Pawara, Bhil, Banjara*	*3,232: 2 revenue :villages, 6 large and many small hamlets*	*20 sq. kms.*	*18 plotholders declared 'eligible'. Grow jowar, cotton, gram and wheat*
19.	Dnyanaganga WLS	Information not available	2 villages		Small patches of private land
20.	Gautala Autramghat Sanctuary	No habitation		0.38 sq. kms.	
21.	Jaikwadi Bird San	No habitation			

22.	*Kalsubai Harish-candrangad WLS*	*Mahadev Koli, Thakur*	*17,066: 32 villages*	*44% of WS is under revenue or private land.*	*Wheat, varai, Jowar, nachni, kolapi, bari, kumed, kali muchcha, indrayani, maize, harbara, rice*
23.	Naigaon Peacock Sanctuary	Information not available	One hamlet		
24.	Nandur Madhmeshar-war Bird San	Mostly Maratha	18,844 (in 1971) from 11 villages		
25.	Painganga WLS	Information not available	22,000 – 38 villages	6.01 sq. kms plus large parts of R.F. plus 35.02 sq. kms. of *abadi* and areas under cultivation.	
26.	*Yaval WL San*	*Pawra, Bhil, Tadvi Bhil*	*2,930 – 7 habitations5*	*0.39 sq. kms.*	
27.	Yedsi Ramling Ghat WLS	Information not available	10,386 – 3 villages		
	Mumbai WL Circle				
28.	*Sanjay Gandhi Rashtriya Udyan*	*Warli, Thakur, Koli, Dhodi, Maratha*	*4,582: 27 revenue villages, 4 tribal dominant villages, 564 tribal houses*	*1.87 sq. kms.*	*Yeoor, Nagla and Chena are old settlements. Practise subsistence agriculture*
29.	Chandoli NP	Maratha, Gavli, Dhangar	8,376 – originally 32 villages		84.29 sq. kms of malki lands. 8 plus 20 villages rehabilitated. 4 remain inside WS.

30.	*Bhimashankar WLS*	*Mahadev Koli (90%), Katkari, Dhangar, Mahar*	*3,181 – 18 villages*	*Settled and shifting cultivation. 35 Eksali plot holders (2.45 sq. kms)*	
31.	Deulgaon-Rehekuri Black Buck Sanctuary	No habitation			
32.	Great Indian Bustard (Extension) Sanctuary	Information not available	791,972		
33.	Karnala Fort Bird San				
34.	Katepurna WLS	Information not available	355 – 3 villages		27% of WS is private. land Agricultural land of these 3 villages plus two others
35.	Koyna WLS	Maratha, Gavli, Dhangar	11,365 : 27 villages	6 cases	
36.	Mayureshwar WLS	Information not available			
37.	Phansad WLS	Information not available	2,256	27 cases, 0.47 sq. kms.	*Eksali* and *dali* holders
38.	Radhanagri WL (Extension) Sanctuary	Maratha, Gavli, Dhangar	20,655 – 65 sites		
39.	Sagareshwar WLS	No habitation			
40.	*Tansa WL (Extension) Sanctuary*	*Warli, Malhar Koli, Mahadev Koli, Katkari,*	*1,099: 5 villages*	*1536 cases: 8.42 sq. kms.*	

(In the above table, the information with respect to tribals is shown in *italics*.)

their forest status. Land settlement has never taken place in these villages. In 1985-86 a survey of the lands was conducted and by virtue of a 1992 Notification, land titles were to be given to the tribals. However, as twenty six of these fall in the submergence area of the Sardar Sarovar Project and 48 are to be included in a Wild life sanctuary, if land titles had been issued, those affected by the projects would have been eligible for the full rehabilitation package. Therefore in 1994, the State government cancelled the earlier Notification. After a prolonged agitation and the intervention of the Mumbai High Court, the Maharashtra government submitted a proposal to transfer 14,790 ha of land within these forest villages to the Revenue department.[107]

5.3 Eviction from 'Private Forests'

In the four Konkan districts of Thane, Raigad, Ratnagiri and Sindhudurg alone, 3.03 lakh ha of agricultural land, affecting more than a lakh of cultivators, mostly Adivasis, had in the 1950s, without the knowledge of most cultivators, been declared to be Private Forests. In 1975, all these lands were with one stroke of a pen acquired and vested in the State. Many of the cultivators are beneficiaries of tenancy legislations, surplus land allottees and non-recorded tenants who are now facing eviction. The process of removing the names of the cultivators from the land records and inserting that of the Forest Department has recently begun.[108] In Shahapur taluka of Thane district, the Forest department has recently begun the process of erecting poles to fence off these lands.

In its 1996 interim order in the *Godavarman* case, the Supreme Court directed that the term 'forest land ....will not only include forest as understood in the dictionary sense, but also any area recorded as forest in the Government record irrespective of the ownership'. Armed with this judgment,

---

107. Campaign for Survival and Dignity, 2003., op. cit.
108. Lobo, Brian. *Land Reforms: Turning the Clock Back*, Economic and Political Weekly, Vol. XXXVII No. 6 Feb 9-15, 2002.

the Forest Department applied pressure on the State Government. The Divisional Commissioner (Revenue), despite not being the competent authority, issued orders to the concerned Tahsildars to make the respective entries in the land records forthwith. Without any verification and due inquiry, the Revenue officers have made mutations in the records. Thus, today in the 7/12 extracts of the tribal farmers, the following remarks have been made: 'Maharashtra Government Forest Department Reserved Forest'. 'Use for non-forest purpose prohibited without prior permission of Central Government', 'The provisions of the Maharashtra Private Forests Acquisition Act are applicable' etc.

5.3 Living and Cultivating in National Parks and Wildlife Sanctuaries

There are many Adivasis who live and hold land that lies within the National Parks and Wildlife Sanctuaries. The status of population and landholdings within these Parks and Sanctuaries is summarized in the following table 8.[109]

From the above, it can be seen that 2 National Parks (NP) and 10 Wild Life Sanctuaries (WLS) (i.e. 30%) do not have people living within the notified areas. Of the 25 WLS, the government had no plans to rehabilitate persons in 76% of the Wildlife sanctuaries. In one NP, the process of Resettlement and Rehabilitation has begun. In Melghat, there are 22 villages in the Tiger Sanctuary. Of these, three villages have been settled near Akot, at Bori, Koho and Kond.[110] The Gavlis received land for land, but not the Korkus. The Government of Maharashtra has in December 2007 sent three proposals to the Central government to declare Critical Tiger Habitats. One more, viz. the Sahyadri Tiger Reserve has also been proposed.

---

109. Pande, Pratibha assisted by Pathak Neema. *National Parks and Sanctuaries in Maharashtra: Reference guide,* Vol I and II and *A State Profile; Individual Profile and Management Status,* Bombay Natural History Society, Mumbai Publication.
110. Interview with Bandya Sane, Paratwadi, Amravatai, May 2007.

6

Land Struggles

Land has been an issue on which the left parties and mass organizations have consistently taken up *andolans or mass movements*. The comparative success of tenancy reform in the Thane district can be attributed to the Warli uprising in the 1940s, when many landlords literally fled the villages. The Kisan Sabha of the undivided Communist Party of India in the 1960s and of the Communist Party of India (Marxist) thereafter, have led many *andolans* in the 1960s and 1970s. The land grab movements of the 1960s were fairly successful in various parts of the state. In the 1970s, the *Bhoomi Sena* in Thane district and the *Shramik Sanghatna* in Dhule district led Adivasi land struggles to regain alienated land. The unrest in the Adivasi areas forced the government to enact the Restoration Acts in 1974 and 1975. In the late 1970s, the *Zabran Zot Andolan* (Movement to Cultivate by Force) emerged around the issue of cultivation on forest land. The *Andolan* which cut across ideological lines was strong in the Vidarbha area, Dhule and Thane districts, though it had constituents in the non-tribal Marathwada area as well. Pressure built up and the government issued a Government Resolution in 1978 to regularize cultivation on forest lands. Later in 1979, the *Andolan* was successful in pressurizing the government to issue an additional Government Resolution to rectify the lacunae in the 1978 G.R. The *Bhoomi Hakk Saurakshan Samiti* which was formed later was an attempt to create a broader all party and mass organization front on the Land issue in both Adivasi and non-Adivasi areas.

Meanwhile, the *Zabran Zot Andolan* was re-named the *Shoshit Jan Andolan* in the mid 1980s. The constituents of *Shoshit Jan Andolan* have independently and collectively undertaken many land struggles. Militant struggles have been organized on the issues of Forest land, *ek-Sali* and *dali* land. In 2002, organizations all over the state, cutting across parties and mass organizations, under the banner of *Karmaveer Dadasaheb Gaekwad Janmashatabdi Bhoomi Hakk Kruti Samiti* forced the government to appoint village level committees to verify claims for regularization of forest encroachments. The issue of non-recorded tenancies has been taken up by many constituent organizations. The Adivasis who have been in possession of these lands for generations, refuse to vacate the lands and instead demand that *Talathis* undertake crop-inspection and make the appropriate entries in the land records. They are also demanding a change in the Tenancy laws such that non-recorded tenants will be able to obtain rights to title. Implementation of the Restoration Acts has been high on the agenda of these organizations. The organizations have been consistently demanding that *gaothans* (homestead land) be extended such that the tribal hamlets also obtain *gaothan* status. In 2001 the *Shoshit Jan Andolan* organized a massive mobilization on the issue of Acquisition of Private Forests. In 2004, the *Shoshit Jan Andolan* organized a Land Rights Conference in an attempt to bring Land Reforms back on the agenda of the government. Following an agitation, the government held a number of parleys but has not initiated any policy changes as yet.

Various struggles have centred on the takeover of tribal lands due to urbanization. Both Adivasis and non-Adivasis have collectively opposed the phenomenon of Special Economic Zones in Raigad district in the recent past.

The implementation of the Forest Rights Act has been high on the agenda of the various tribal organizations, but even so, implementation has been tardy in most parts of the state. The struggle continues to implement the Act in a proper manner.

Over the years, the various organizations have resorted both to legal and extra-legal strategies. A number of Public Interest Litigations have been filed.

7

Conclusion

The Land issue in the Adivasi areas is getting more and more complex. The continuous onslaught by capital is slowly but surely eating into the survival base of the Adivasis. Land Reform legislations had the opposite effect to what was intended. Even the Restoration Acts have had very meager success. There appears to be a trend towards the withdrawal of the protective legislations. Now that Act 14/75 is not being extended, it seems likely that amendments will be made to make Act 35/74 ineffective. The Special Notification for the Development of Hill Stations is a pointer in that direction. While the phenomenon of Special Economic Zones is resulting in direct alienation of Adivasi lands in a relatively small measure, much larger indirect alienation is occurring through infrastructure development for SEZs in the hinterland. And anyway, the implementation of even progressive legislations works against the Adivasi. In the absence of strong peoples' movements, the decimation of Adivasi communities is a fait accompli. Even where strong peoples' movements exist, the dice is so loaded that the future looks very uncertain.

At the same time, the Adivasi communities themselves are getting more stratified, leading to a breakdown of traditional communitarian ties and attachment to land. The emerging elite within the community is trying to consolidate its landholdings. Elected tribal representatives including MLAs and MPs are amassing lands in their areas.

The forests hold the key to the future of the Adivasi areas. The implementation of the Scheduled Tribes and Other Forest Dwellers (Recognition of Forest Rights) Act 2006 is on the agenda of many Adivasi organizations. However limiting its implementation only to land rights will not lead to any significant change in the situation. Take-over of forests must go hand-in-hand with cultivation on forest land. It is only then that the real land issue in Adivasi area—Self-rule of Adivasi homelands—will be addressed.